BRITAIN AND NATO'S NORTHERN FLANK

Also by Geoffrey Till

AIR POWER AND THE ROYAL NAVY
*MARITIME STRATEGY AND THE NUCLEAR AGE
*THE SEA IN SOVIET STRATEGY (*with Bryan Ranft*)
*THE FUTURE OF BRITISH SEAPOWER (*editor*)

*Also published by Macmillan

Britain and NATO's Northern Flank

Edited by

Geoffrey Till
Principal Lecturer
Department of History and International Affairs
The Royal Naval College, Greenwich

M
MACMILLAN
PRESS

© Geoffrey Till 1988

All rights reserved. No reproduction, copy or transmission of this publication may be made without written permission.

No paragraph of this publication may be reproduced, copied or transmitted save with written permission or in accordance with the provisions of the Copyright Act 1956 (as amended), or under the terms of any licence permitting limited copying issued by the Copyright Licensing Agency, 33–4 Alfred Place, London WC1E 7DP.

Any person who does any unauthorised act in relation to this publication may be liable to criminal prosecution and civil claims for damages.

First published 1988

Published by
THE MACMILLAN PRESS LTD
Houndmills, Basingstoke, Hampshire RG21 2XS
and London
Companies and representatives
throughout the world

Typeset by Wessex Typesetters
(Division of The Eastern Press Ltd)
Frome, Somerset

Printed in Hong Kong

British Library Cataloguing in Publication Data
Britain and NATO's northern flank.
1. North Atlantic Treaty Organization
2. Security, International 3. Europe,
Northern—Strategic aspects
I. Till, Geoffrey
355′.031′091821   UA646.3
ISBN 0-333-43931-7

Contents

List of Figures vii
List of Tables viii
List of Maps ix
List of Abbreviations x
Notes on the Contributors xii
Preface xv

PART I   THE POLITICAL AND ECONOMIC CONTEXT
1   The Political and Economic Context 3
    Clive Archer
2   A Swedish View 21
    Bo Huldt

    Conference Discussion 29

PART II   SECURITY IN NORTHERN EUROPE
3   The Security Pattern in Northern Europe: A Norwegian View 35
    Johan Jørgen Holst
4   The Security Context: A Soviet View 51
    Malcom Mackintosh

    Conference Discussion 58

PART III   BRITAIN AND THE NORTH
5   An Overview of British Defence Policy in the North 65
    Sir William Staveley
6   A Change in British Priorities? 74
    Jonathan Alford

    Conference Discussion 83

PART IV   THE SEA CAMPAIGN
7   Maritime–Air Operations in the North: American Perspectives 89
    Robert S. Wood

Contents

8   A German View   103
F. U. Kupferschmidt

9   The Maritime Strategy: A Norwegian View   110
Thor Nikolaisen

10   A British View   114
Geoffrey Till

Conference Discussion   124

PART V THE LAND CAMPAIGN

11   Land–Air Operations in the North   131
Sir Jeremy Moore

12   The Northern Flank: The Air Dimension   140
John Price

13   The Military Importance of the Northern Flank: A Dutch View   146
A. C. Lamers

14   The Security of the Northern Flank: A Danish View   151
B. Fr. Lindhardt

Conference Discussion   159

PART VI OPTIONS AND CONCLUSIONS

15   Future Policy Options   165
Sir James Eberle

Conference Discussion   175

Concluding Remarks   178
Lawrence Freedman

Index   185

List of Figures

12.1 Position of Commander-in-Chief, Allied Forces Northern Europe, in Allied Command Europe   143

List of Tables

4.1	Strength of the Soviet Northern and Baltic Fleets	52
4.2	Armed Forces of Scandinavia	53
5.1	Strength of the Royal Navy	66
12.1	Allied Forces Northern Europe	141
12.2	The Northern Region of ACE	141

List of Maps

1. Scandinavia — 6
2. Arctic ice lines — 37
3. Svalbard and the Barents Sea — 47

List of Abbreviations

ACE	Allied Command Europe
AFNORTH	Allied Forces North
AMF	Allied Mobile Force
ASW	Anti-submarine warfare
BALTAP	Baltic Approaches Command
CAST–BG	Canadian Air–Sea Transportable Brigade
CHQ	Guided missile helicopter cruiser
CINCEASTLANT	Commander-in-Chief Eastern Atlantic
CINCHAN	Commander-in-Chief Channel
CINCNORTH	Commander-in-Chief Northern Command
CG	Guided missile cruiser
CL	Light cruiser
COBs	Co-located operating (air) bases
COMBALTAP	Commander of Baltic Approaches Command
CONMAROPS	Concept of Maritime Operations
CV	Aircraft carrier, conventionally-powered
CVBG	Aircraft carrier battle group
DDG	Guided missile destroyer
EC	European Communities
FFG	Guided missile frigate
FFL	Light frigate
FPB	Fast patrol boat
GIN	Greenland–Iceland–Norway gap
GIUK	Greenland–Iceland–UK gap
GDP	General defence plan (Gross domestic product)
LEMD	Leningrad Military District
LPD	Amphibious assault transport dock
LRMP	Long-range maritime patrol
LST	Amphibious vehicle landing ship
LSM	Medium amphibious assault landing ship
MAB	(United States) Marine Amphibious Brigade
MCM	Mine countermeasures
NATO	North Atlantic Treaty Organization
NEC	Northern Europe Command
NNFZ	Nordic nuclear weapons-free zone
SACEUR	Supreme Allied Commander Europe

List of Abbreviations

SACLANT	Supreme Allied Commander Atlantic
SAM	Surface-to-air missile
SBS	Special Boat Squadron
SDI	Strategic defence initiative
SLBM	Submarine-launched ballistic missile
SLOCs	Sea lines of communication
SONOR	Southern Norway Command
SONUS	Sound surveillance (of submarines) system
SS	Diesel-powered submarine
SSB	Diesel-powered ballistic missile-firing submarine
SSBN	Nuclear-powered ballistic missile-firing submarine
SSGN	Nuclear-powered cruise missile-firing submarine
SSM	Surface-to-surface missile
SSN	Nuclear-powered attack submarine
STANAVFORLANT	Standing Naval Force Atlantic
TASMO	Tactical air support, maritime operations
TVD	(Soviet) theatre of strategic action
UKMF	UK mobile force
UK/NL L(A)F	UK/Netherlands landing (or amphibious) force
UNCLOS	United Nations Convention on the Law of the Sea
USAF	United States Air Force
USMC	United States Marine Corps
USN	United States Navy
WEU	Western European Union

Notes on the Contributors

Colonel Jonathan Alford was until his death in August 1986 Deputy Director of the International Institute for Strategic Studies.

Clive Archer is the Deputy Director, Centre for Defence Studies, University of Aberdeen, a post he has held since 1982. He is chairman of the Royal Institute of International Affairs Study Group on Northern Waters.

Admiral Sir James Eberle, GCB, became Director of the Royal Institute of International Affairs in January 1984. He retired from the Active List of the Royal Navy in 1983, his last appointment having been as Commander-in-Chief Naval Home Command, and prior to that the Commander-in-Chief Fleet.

Professor Lawrence Freedman is head of the War Studies Department at King's College, London. Amongst his most recent works are *Britain and Nuclear Weapons* and *The Evolution of Nuclear Strategy*.

Dr Johan Jørgen Holst began the 1986 conference as Director of the Norwegian Institute of International Affairs, and ended it as Defence Minister in the Norwegian government.

Bo Huldt is Deputy Director of the Swedish Institute of International Affairs, Stockholm.

Commander F. U. Kupferschmidt is Assistant Naval Attaché at the Embassy of the Federal Republic of Germany in London. Prior to this he served as Executive Officer in a frigate and before that in the Ministry of Defence, Bonn.

Major-General Adrien Lamers, RNLMC (Rtd), retired in 1977, having served for over three years as Commandant of the Royal Netherlands Marine Corps, where he joined after the Liberation in 1945. Since retirement, he has been a military member of a working group studying and discussing the independence of the Netherlands Antilles and President of the Royal Netherlands Naval Association 'Onze Vloot'.

Notes on the Contributors

B. Fr. Lindhardt is recipient of a NATO Defence Fellowship for a study of BALTAP reinforcement and is one of Denmark's leading defence analysts.

Malcolm Mackintosh, author of *Juggernaut*, an analysis of the Soviet Armed Forces, is Assistant Secretary in the Cabinet Office.

Major General Sir Jeremy Moore, KCB, OBE, MC, commanded the Royal Marine Commando Forces 1979–82 and was Commander Land Forces in the Falklands in 1982; he retired into civilian life in 1983.

Captain Thor Nikolaisen RNON is currently the Norwegian Defence Attaché in London. Before that he served as Adviser to the Royal Norwegian Ministry of Defence on Military and Security Policy Matters. His previous appointments have included work at the Norwegian National Institute for International Affairs.

Air Vice-Marshall John Price, CBE (Rtd), is the Administration Manager for Clyde Petroleum PLC. His last tour of duty before retiring in 1984 was as Assistant Chief of Air Staff (Operations).

Admiral Sir William Staveley, GCB, ADC, was appointed First Sea Lord and Chief of the Naval Staff, and First and Principal Aide-de-Camp to Her Majesty the Queen in August 1985, in succession to Admiral of the Fleet Sir John Fieldhouse. His previous appointment was Commander-in-Chief Fleet, when he also assumed the NATO appointments of Allied Commander-in-Chief Channel and Commander-in-Chief Eastern Atlantic Area.

Dr Geoffrey Till is member of the Department of History and International Affairs of the Royal Naval College, Greenwich, and also teaches in the Department of War Studies, King's College, London. He is the author of *Maritime Strategy and the Nuclear Age* and *The Sea in Soviet Strategy* (with Bryan Ranft), and the editor of *The Future of British Sea Power*.

Dr Robert S. Wood is Dean of the Center for Naval Warfare Studies at the Naval War College, Newport, Rhode Island. He has been Professor of Government and Foreign Affairs at the University of Virginia and is currently a consultant to the White House, the Department of Defense and the Department of State.

Preface

In November 1983 a conference was held at the Royal Over-Seas League in London on 'The Future of British Sea Power'. Successful though it undoubtedly was, the organizers – the Department of War Studies, King's College, London, the Royal Naval College, Greenwich, and the Navy Department at the Ministry of Defence – all thought the conference left much to be said and thought about. The wide scope of the material covered meant there was inevitably a high level of generality. Next time, the organizers decided, the conference would address a narrower issue.

Since that time the Soviet Navy has continued to make steady progress. The Soviet Northern Fleet, in particular, made itself significantly visible in some spectacular exercises in 1983, 1984 and 1985 and Soviet submarines began appearing in all kinds of unexpected places. At the same time the United States Navy started to attract a good deal of attention in Europe with its espousal of the idea of 'Forward Operations' in the waters to the north of Europe. All this meant that NATO's Northern Flank has become a major issue of concern in defence and academic circles.

In order to facilitate the consequent debate about what was at issue, about what the results might be for Britain, and indeed about what Britain should be doing as a result of it all, the War Studies Department at King's College decided to hold another conference, on the subject of 'Britain and the Northern Flank'. In order to ensure that the participants were not naval officers simply preaching to other naval officers and their associates (often the fate of maritime conferences), the conference organizers made every effort to lure other service officers, Scandinavians and Americans to the proceedings. The conference was held in May 1986 at the Royal Festival Hall and was launched by the First Sea Lord, Admiral Sir William Staveley.

The pages which follow are the product of that conference. At the end of each Part there is a Conference Discussion section which attempts to summarize the reactions to the papers delivered. The quality of the discussion owes much to the inspired conference chairmanship of Professors Bryan Ranft and Peter Nailor. Of course a great deal more was said than is reported, but I hope that these sections will capture at least a flavour of the response. It should not be assumed that the editor, the King's College Department of War Studies, the

Ministry of Defence or any other body or persons necessarily agree with any of the ideas expressed in these sections. Also, contributors are responsible for the contents of their own chapters but no more; I would like to thank them all for their efforts and their patience, then and since. I would also like to thank Professor Lawrence Freedman for providing the inspiration behind the conference. Without the, as usual, sterling efforts of the naval team of Captain John Dunt, Commander Richard Hirst and 2/0 Allie Husk neither conference nor book would have been possible.

But really in endeavours such as this it is the back-up of secretaries and typists which makes all possible, so I would like to acknowledge with real gratitude the help of Wendy Everett in the Department of War Studies and Kathy Mason in the Department of History and International Affairs. Above all, perhaps, I would like to thank Jean Taylor and her gallant ladies in the typing pool at the Royal Naval College, Greenwich, for their tremendous efforts in tackling the enormous typing effort such an enterprise requires. Without them, this maritime expedition would have foundered before it even reached the Northern Flank.

Royal Naval College GEOFFREY TILL
Greenwich

Part I
The Political and Economic Context

1 The Political and Economic Context
Clive Archer

The military situation in the Northern Flank – and, indeed, the security pattern in Northern Europe described in other chapters of this book – depends, of necessity, primarily on factors external to the region. Examinations of the defence of the area have stressed the contribution of American and British forces, and Johan Jørgen Holst (Chapter 3) has described its regional security as being 'woven into various dimensions of the East–West military competition'.[1] However, certain political and economic elements in the region itself are worthy of examination as they help to explain the security policies (including the defence postures) of the Nordic states which are so central to the area. They also pose choices in the future for the governments of those countries.

After a brief introduction, this chapter will examine the economic situation in the region, will then turn to political activities there and will finally elucidate some of the difficult decisions facing Nordic governments.

INTRODUCTION

The Northern Flank, in the NATO context, has come to include Denmark and Norway and the surrounding maritime area from the Greenland–Iceland–(Faeroes)–United Kingdom (GIUK) Gap eastwards to the Norwegian Sea, the Barents and the Baltic. This chapter will concentrate on the Nordic countries as they form a barrier between the two Superpowers in the north.

The Nordic countries include five stable, wealthy democracies – Denmark, Finland, Iceland, Norway and Sweden. There are also three home-rule territories – Greenland, the Faroe Islands (both part of Denmark) and the Aaland Islands (part of Finland) – and the important strategic Norwegian islands of Jan Mayen in the North Atlantic and Svalbard, to the north of the Barents Sea.

The Nordic countries are often regarded as 'small states' but their geographical size – Greenland alone being the world's largest island – and importance should be remembered. However, all are sparsely populated[2] and are, more precisely, 'small powers'[3] albeit ones with important strategic positions and even leading roles in particular commercial areas such as shipping and communications.

As small powers, the Nordic countries have had to adapt themselves to the international situation.[4] It has been suggested that a static foreign policy behaviour can be determined by its *influence capability* 'representing the degree to which an actor can affect or manipulate his external environment' and its *stress sensitivity*, that is 'the degree to which societal structures are affected by changes in the external environment'.[5] The Nordic countries seem to have a fairly limited influence capability which they have to utilize judiciously, and their societies seen to be comparatively little affected by outside events, though this has been changing.

ECONOMIC SITUATION

One area where the Nordic states find themselves dependent on the outside world is that of economic activity. The imports and exports of the Nordic states, when measured on a *per capita* basis, were substantially higher than those of the European Communities (EC), let alone the USA, Japan or Comecon.[6] However, the five Nordic countries are not without resources, neither are they unproductive. In 1983 natural gas production was over a million terajoules (compared to the EC's 5.9 million terajoules), crude petroleum 27.6 million tons (EC: 105.4 million tons), iron ore 11 million tons (EC: 5.7 million tons), sawnwood 36 million m^3 (EC: 18 million m^3), electric energy 12 kWh *per capita* (EC: 4.75 kWh *per capita*), merchant fleet 30 million GRT (EC: 95.6 million GRT). Nordic Gross Domestic Product (GDP) *per capita* in 1982 was $11 648 compared with $8706 for the EC, Japan's $9026 and the USAs $13 106.[7]

The economies of each of the five Nordic states have similarities of structure. Sweden has a large service and commercial sector (54 per cent of economically active population in 1980) compared with that of manufacturing and mining (26 per cent), is a net energy importer and had a 2 per cent annual average growth in GDP in the 1970s. Norway also has a large service and commercial sector (48 per cent in 1980) compared with 26 per cent of the economically active population in mining and manufacturing, but is a net energy exporter and managed a

4.7 per cent annual average growth in its GDP in the 1970s. The equivalent figures for Denmark are 55 per cent in service and commerce, 20 per cent in mining and manufacturing and a 2.3 per cent GDP average growth figure. Finland and Iceland have certain common features – 43 per cent in service and commerce, 27 per cent in mining and manufacturing in both cases – though the 13 per cent each has in agriculture, forestry and fishing was distributed differently, with the first two areas taking the major sector in Finland and fishing being dominant in Iceland. The rates of growth in their GDPs in the 1970s were 3.7 per cent for Finland and 5.2 per cent for Iceland.[8] The trade of all the Nordic countries is directed primarily to and from the OECD countries, with the EC being the best customer and supplier in all cases. However, Iceland has a sizeable trade with the Soviet bloc (about 11 per cent of imports – mainly oil) and with the USA (about 29 per cent of exports – mainly fish), whilst Finland sells between 20 and 26 per cent of its exports to the Soviet Union and receives a similar share of its imports from there.[9]

The 1980s have seen mixed results for the Nordic economies. All have suffered labour disputes unusual for these havens of industrial peace and the then energy importers – all except Norway – were hit by the rise in oil prices 1979–81. Icelandic inflation went into three figures; Sweden's economic position was salvaged by an unexpected devaluation in 1982; oil dominated Norway's economy and became more important in that of Denmark; Finnish economic stability became a source of admiration. Questions were asked in all countries as to whether an increased proportion of resources could be continually devoted to government expenditure.[10]

The sudden fall in oil prices in early 1986 further divided the Nordic states between energy importers and exporters. At one end of the spectrum, Norway was plunged into economic difficulties, made worse by industrial action offshore in April 1986. It has been estimated that the oil price decrease, taken with the falling value of the dollar, could reduce the Norwegian government's tax income by some 30 billion NOK (about £3 billion) which is equivalent to the 1986 expenditure of the Ministries of Defence, Communications and Justice. It is reckoned that the government would have had to increase VAT by about 1 per cent for every dollar per barrel the price of oil falls in order to compensate for such losses.[11] As in the United Kingdom, the non-oil economy will receive succour from falling world oil prices, but this sector is much smaller in Norway than in Britain. Iceland lies at the other end of the spectrum: it largely benefited from the oil price

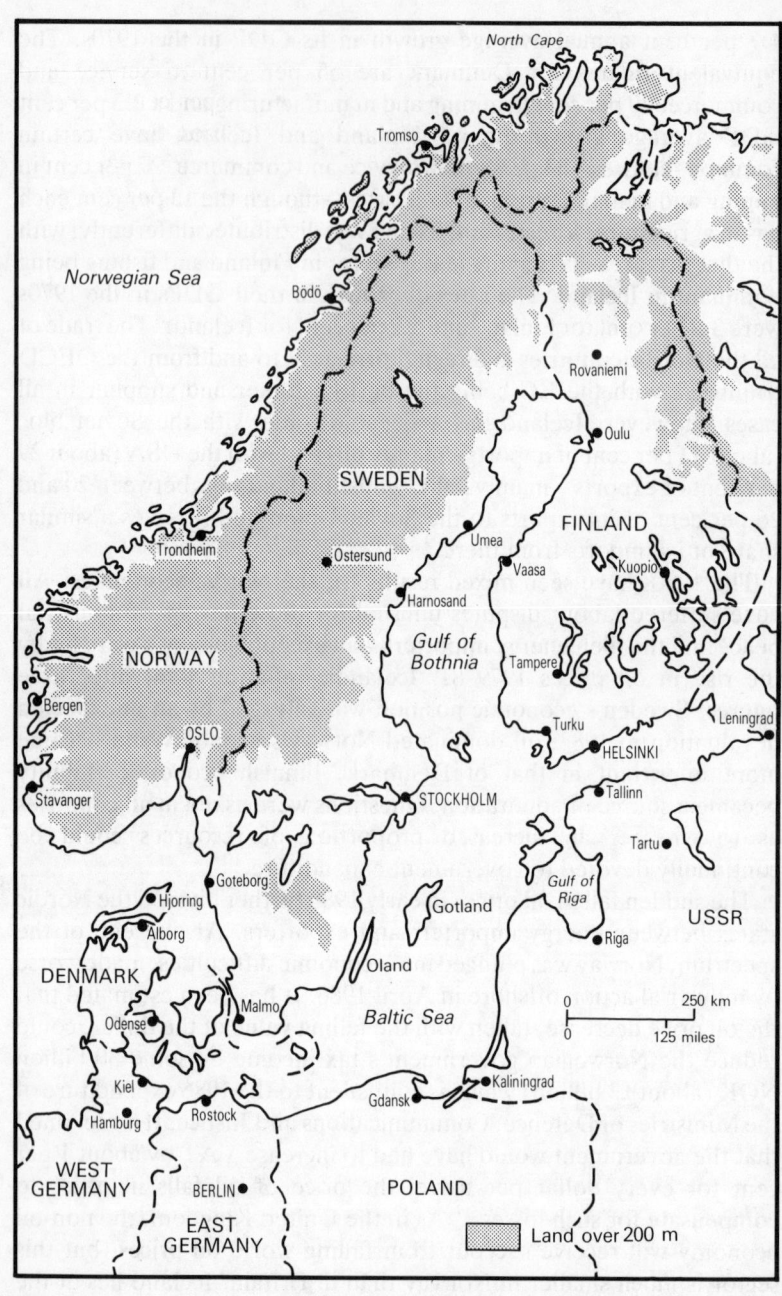

Map 1 Scandinavia

reduction. Earlier in 1986 it was estimated that this movement and the increase in fish prices abroad could improve the trade balance by 2 billion Icelandic kroner (about £33 million) or 11 per cent of GNP. Sweden also saw a positive effect both on its inflation figure and its balance of payments. The situation in Finland was more complicated as importing Soviet petroleum has been the way of getting payment for Finnish exports of ships and engineering equipment to the Soviet Union, a bilateral trade which has political as well as economic significance. Increased oil prices meant a greater Finnish export effort (and more work at home) to pay for oil imports from the USSR; lower prices could mean a lower demand for Finnish exports, not only to the Soviet Union but also to two other important customers, Norway and Britain. The oil price fall has not been an unmixed blessing for Denmark, which has a number of long-term contracts for oil purchases and is also a burgeoning North Sea petroleum product producer in its own right.

It can thus be seen in economic matters, the Nordic countries' 'influence capability' is fairly low – they tend to be the objects of world economic events, and have to adapt as best they can to new conditions. Having fairly well developed governmental systems, they seem to do this better than most states, but over recent years their 'stress sensitivity' has grown, with their societies being increasingly affected by outside economic changes. Efforts to bring the Nordic states together in a single economic unit have failed in the past,[12] though the countries have found some protection against the world economic changes within EFTA (Finland, Iceland, Norway, Sweden) and the EC (Denmark, and the other countries also have trade agreements with the EC).

POLITICAL SITUATION

The five Nordic countries have had a number of factors in common which have also marked them out from the rest of Europe – they have never had any significant colonies, nor have they been colonized themselves (as were the Balkan states);[13] feudalism was of limited influence and they were able to industrialize rapidly; the Nordic nations are reasonably equal in size, thus helping regional co-operation. However, two Nordic states – Denmark and Finland – have bordered Great Powers and two others – Iceland and Norway – have felt the strong maritime influence of Great Powers, and the area has had only limited success in keeping outside involvement at bay.[14] This short description leads to two conclusions about the Nordic countries' political situation: it is one that should encourage co-operation between like-minded nations; it is also one that allows domestic political attitudes little influence over the wider events that determine the strategic future of these states.

Nordic co-operation is a paradox; it is an apparent success with a number of failures to its name. The relationship of the countries involved has been described as one where contacts are plentiful but commitments are few.[15] Whilst the institutions of the European Communities are intrusive, politicized and often *dirigiste*, those of Nordic co-operation tend to be more consensual, functional and permissive, building as they do on the similarities of the Nordic countries. Such institutions have been least successful in areas of noted policy difference – for example, defence policy – or where connections with third countries have proved stronger than intraNordic ties, as has been the case in trade links. Still, there does exist a meeting of parliamentarians – the Nordic Council – and of government representatives – the Nordic Council of Ministers – as well as a host of other governmental and non-governmental organizations ranging from secretariats[16] to voluntary associations.[17] Opinion polls have shown that this network of Nordic co-operation reflects a strong popular bond between the Nordic peoples, though not one that excludes links with other countries.[18] In particular limited areas Nordic co-operation has been successfully used as an 'influence multiplier' for the Nordic countries acting on the world stage. This was noticeably the case in the GATT 'Kennedy Round' negotiations when the Nordic states were involved as a bloc and in Norden's aid policy.[19] Whilst it is true that the Nordic countries have not co-operated institutionally in their defense policies, it should be remembered that there is an assumption of Nordic co-operation over issues that have a wider security import (such as UN peacekeeping, aid to the Third World), and that there is a background of Nordic opinion and organizations active in the general area of peace and security.[20] The existence of Nordic institutions has been seen by some as a resource to the utilized in order to heighten Nordic 'influence capability' in defence matters, or at least to attenuate the worst aspects of their 'stress sensitivity' to outside international strategic events.

Before examining the consequences of this train of thought, it is necessary to mention the political background in each of the Nordic states in the 1980s. In case it is still thought that government in the

Nordic region is an unrelieved social democratic landscape, populated by rational decision-makers tilling the soil of welfare statism, it should be mentioned that by mid-1986 there were two centre-right governments in the Nordic region, one centre-left and two purely Social Democrat governments. Only in Iceland and Finland do the governing parties have an overall majority in parliament. A more tragic element of modern politics has also struck the Nordic states – Prime Minister Palme of Sweden became the only post-war European premier to fall to the assassin's bullet and in 1985 Atli Dam, Faeroese head of government, was stabbed as he addressed the *Lagting* (Faeroese parliament).

Finland provides the one example in the Nordic region of a mixture of the parliamentary and presidential systems. The Finnish president still has important executive powers, including those dealing with foreign and security policies. During the 1960s and early 1970s, Finland's political system looked problematic with a large Communist Party which had government portfolios, and a somewhat excessive dependence in foreign relations on the ageing president, Kekkonen. The transition from Kekkonen to President Koivisto has been made smoothly and in 1986 the Centre–Social Democrat–Swedish Party–Smallholders' coalition has a sizeable parliamentary majority. The Communist party has been reduced in size, has left government and has almost completely split between Moscow-line and Eurocommunist supporters.

With the limits allowed by the Paris Peace Treaty of 1947, and of budgetary constraint, the Finns have built up their defence forces. In the 3rd Paliamentary Defence Committee's *Report* for the period covering 1982–6, an annual real increase of 3.8 per cent in defence expenditure was recommended and attention was turned to a greater defence presence in Northern Finland, better equipment for the air force and the need to defend Finnish air-space against intrusion from sea-launched cruise missiles.[21]

Sweden after the September 1985 election had a continuation of the Social Democrat minority government, in power since 1982. As before, it depended on the Left Party Communists (VPK) for its parliamentary majority but the three opposition parties – Liberals, Conservatives and Centre – together had more seats than those of the Social Democrats alone. This meant the government was even more dependent on its leftist partner: whereas previously the Social Democrats could still win a division if the VPK abstained, it was no longer the case after September 1985. Before his death, Olof Palme, aware of this new situation, made overtures to the Liberal and Centre parties. It should also be noted that much legislation in Sweden is passed with all-party or cross-party support.

It has certainly been the case that Sweden's security policy has received the support of all parties outside the VPK, though Social Democrat handling of international security events in the 1982–5 parliament was often strongly criticized by the Conservatives. In February 1985, the opposition parties introduced a motion of no confidence in the then Foreign Minister, Lennart Bodström, who had made some offhand remarks about both the submarine threat to Sweden and a possible visit by him to Moscow ('We'll first win the election. I don't see that this will be done by such a visit').[22] Despite this, defence and foreign policies were not election issues and all the parties (except VPK) united in their support of Sweden's traditional alliance-free stance. After the election the Foreign Ministry was placed in safer and less controversial hands than Mr Bodström's, in the form of former Minister of Social Affairs, Sten Andersson. With Palme's death, Ingvar Carlsson has become Prime Minister and it remains to be seen how he takes to the international stage. Whilst Swedish policy has not changed, it is clear that Carlsson will not be able to emulate Palme's high profile on matters such as nuclear disarmament, the Iran–Iraq War and Third World questions. At the international level, Sweden has been left with an empty chair.

The election in *Norway* in September 1985 saw the return of a centre-right coalition government which had been in power – in one form or another – since 1981 when Mr Kaare Willoch became the first post-war Conservative Norwegian prime minister.[23] In British terms, the Norwegian Conservatives are distinctly 'wet' and their policies in government have been further watered down by the presence of their coalition partners, the Centre Party and the Christian People's Party. The September election gave the Labour Party and the Socialist Left Party 77 seats and the Coalition parties 78 seats, leaving the then government dependent on the votes of the two free-market Progress Party MPs for their majority. On most issues, the Progress Party obliged by voting with the Coalition or by abstaining. However, the fall in the oil price made its mark politically. The centre-right government brought in an 'Easter Package' to cope with the potential loss of oil income but found this opposed on grounds of equity by the socialist opposition parties, whilst the Progress Party was unable to support a petrol taxation increase. This led to the parliamentary defeat of Mr Willoch's government on 1 May 1986 and its replacement by a minority Labour Party administration led by Mrs Gro Harlem Brundtland. In order to survive, the new government either has to adopt consensus policies that will not be opposed by the centre-right parties, or (less likely) will have to obtain the consistent support of one of the centre parties. Mrs Brundtland has indicated that Norway's security policy will continue as before and the appointments of Knut Frydenlund as Foreign Minister and Johan Jørgen Holst as Defence Minister seem to confirm this.

During the election campaign, Norwegian security policy surprisingly became an issue, though not one with much voter impact. The Norwegian Labour Party has traditionally had a strong pro-NATO leadership: indeed it was the then Labour Foreign Minister, Halvard Lange, who helped to found the Organization. However, the Party has also had a more pacifist left wing, much of which broke away in the early 1960s to form the Socialist People's Party (now the Socialist Left Party). The Labour Party leader, Gro Harlem Brundtland, has taken the traditional line on NATO on many defense issues but her deputy, Einar Fjørde, is more in the pacifist mould. He came under attack from the Conservatives during the election campaign and in the end Mrs Brundtland was obliged to announce that Mr Fjørde would not become either Defence or Foreign Minister in any government she formed. Whilst the Conservatives (and their allies) were returned to power and thus could claim that their attack on Fjørde – and on Labour's security policy record generally[24] – produced electoral benefits, there was a price to pay. In June 1984 the government parties and Labour had re-established the broad consensus on security policy that had long existed in Norway but which had come under pressure in the early 1980s. The subsequent attack by the Conservatives on Labour for being untrustworthy on defence has not helped further co-operation over security policy, should the Labour Party get a majority at the next election in September 1989. Also, the Centre Party and Christian People's Party are less 'tough' on defence than the Conservatives and a handful of their parliamentarians are known to sympathize more with the Labour line on such issues as nuclear freeze, paying NATO infrastructure support for the Dual Track Programme, and support for SDI-related research. The Conservatives had to go along with policies on the first issue supported because the Labour Party found support for their line among the centre parties.

Norway's Chief of Defence, General Bull Hansen, perhaps did not choose the best time in November 1985 to ask for a real increase in defence expenditure of some 7–8 per cent to start with, followed by an annual 6–7 per cent increase until the turn of the century. Given the new parliamentary situation and the economic effect on Norway of oil price decreases, the General will be lucky to get the 3.5 per cent increase mentioned by the then Conservative chairman of the *Storting*'s (parliament's) Finance Committee, Anders Talleraas.[25]

Denmark has a complicated parliamentary situation. A centre-right government was re-elected in January 1984 but, as before, they depended on the social–liberal Radical Party for their majority over the socialist parties. The coalition parties – Conservatives, Liberals, Centre Democrats and Christian People's Party – have 78 out of the 179 seats in parliament but can normally rely on five right-wing MPs and perhaps two of the four Greenlandic and Faeroese members. To outvote the socialist bloc (84 seats), the government needs either the abstention (but preferably the support) of the ten Radical MPs.

The problem is that the Radicals support the government of Conservative Paul Schlüter on most economic issues but not on most security questions when they vote with the socialist parties (Social Democrats, Socialist People's Party, Left Socialist, a Greenlander and a Faroese). This has led to a government that does not have a parliamentary majority for its own security policy and thus has to reserve its position at meetings of NATO (and sometimes the EC) and even vote contrary to its wishes at the UN (e.g. on the nuclear freeze issue). The 'alternative security policy majority' in parliament has even forced the government to stop making payments to the NATO infrastructure programme for cruise and Pershing missiles. The Social Democrats have now developed a plan for the reorganization of Danish defence to create a 'non-offensive defence'. This involves an increase in the number of soldiers (including the Home Guard), and a decrease in the number of naval and air force personnel. Frigates and submarines would be phased out, with the emphasis switched to coastal batteries and mines. The aim would be not to provoke any potential adversary but to raise the cost of invading Denmark.

Despite all this, there is still a consensus of sorts on defence in Denmark. When it comes to agreeing the defence budget, the governing parties have sought compromise with the Social Democrats and together (excluding the Radicals, assorted socialists and right wingers) have drawn up Defence Agreements which have allowed for a modest replacement programme for the Danish armed forces.[26]

Little attention is often given to the Danish North Atlantic islands – Greenland and the Faeroes. This in unfortunate as they have seen important political changes over the past ten years and are situated in strategically important areas. Both send two representatives to the Danish parliament (*Folketing*) but both also have Home Rule assemblies and administrations.

Greenland's political development has been particularly rapid recently. In 1953 its status was changed from one of Danish colony to that of a county within the Danish kingdom. Though in the 1972 referendum Greenlanders overwhelmingly voted against membership of the European Communities, their constitutional status meant that as part of Denmark they joined the EC, unlike the Faeroese who already had Home Rule. The response to this and to the handing out of oil concessions in Greenland by the Danish government in 1975, was a move towards autonomy by the 50 000 Greenlanders. The *Folketing* passed the Greenland Home Rule Act in November 1978 and it was accepted by referendum in Greenland. The Home Rule assembly and administration, established in May 1979, have taken over most of domestic policy, though exploration of natural resources is a joint responsibility with Copenhagen and defence and foreign affairs matters remain in the hands of the Danish government which is, however, obliged to consult the Greenland administration on matters affecting Greenland. Since the introduction of Home Rule, Greenland has had a broadly moderate socialist government under the leadership of Pastor Jonathan Motzfeldt. Its main international task has been to negotiate, through the Danish government, Greenland's movement from being a part of the EC to having Overseas Countries and Territories status, which was successfully done by 1 February 1985.

Greenland has been (and still is) of security importance to the West.[27] Most important are the two US Space Command defence areas at Thule and Sondrestrom.[28] Whilst the US deals directly with the Copenhagen government on base questions, the existence of these two areas *has* impinged on Greenlandic politics. The moving of an Inuit community from the Thule area, the crash landing near Thule of a B-52 with nuclear weapons on board in 1968, and the accusation that facilities in the defence areas were servicing an American 'First Strike' policy have all been used by the left wing in Denmark and Greenland in their campaigns against the US presence. More moderate Greenlanders have used planning regulations for new DEW-line sites and the question of rent for the areas as levers to get more Greenlandic involvement in the defence area question. On the whole, the Greenlandic administration has taken a cool but practical attitude on the issue.[29]

The Faeroe Islands have had an autonomous status within the Danish kingdom since 1948. Their Home Rule administration deals with internal affairs and, as with Greenland, foreign and defence matters are dealt with by Copenhagen, with the proviso that the Faeroese Home Rule government will be consulted on matters affecting the islands. At present there are six political parties in the Faeroes: one wants independence, one an independent republic, one desires greater autonomy, one wishes to retain the status quo, another is social-democratic and the sixth is a fishermen's party.

Like their Greenlandic equivalents, Faeroese governments have interested themselves in the NATO communications installations on their islands. Since November 1984 the Faeroes has had a Home Rule government of Social Democrats and Republicans led by Atli Dam who, when Chief Minister in the 1974 government, tried to use the presence of NATO stations on the island as a negotiating card in fisheries talks with the EC.

This Faeroese ploy was one that they copied from *Iceland*. Icelandic governments from the 1950s through to the 1970s became expert at 'linkage politics', whereby they used the presence of the US base at Keflavik to lever concessions on fishing limits out of other NATO countries, primarily the British. Since then, Icelandic governments have taken a fresh look at the defence question.

It used to be the case that when the liberal Progressives led the Icelandic government more pressure was likely to be placed on the US base at Keflavik, with demands that its men and television should not pollute Icelandic culture, or (in 1956) that the base should be closed. In 1971 when the Communist-dominated People's Alliance was also in government with the Progressives, closure moves were started but did not get far, and in a similar government in 1978 the call was merely for no expansion of the base. By the 1980s, all the political parties except the People's Alliance (PA) had come to accept the US presence and even the PA was not prepared to make its abolition a *sine qua non* of participation in government.

The new Independence (Conservative) Party – Progressive coalition formed after the April 1983 elections took an entirely new approach towards international security questions, led by Geir Hallgrimsson, Foreign Minister until January 1986 and a former Prime Minister. Iceland has no armed forces and is defended by the Americans in the guise of the Iceland Defence Force (IDF). After the 1983 election, the new government encouraged greater Icelandic involvement in its own – and Allied – defence. It has created a Defence Division in its Ministry of Foreign Affairs, accepted the updating of the IDF's resources and the building of facilities financed by the NATO infrastructure fund, participated in the work of the NATO Military Committee and encouraged the involvement of other NATO countries in the defense of Iceland and the surrounding area.[30]

In summary, recent developments in the politics of the Nordic countries have produced a variety of governments. Those in the core Scandinavian states – Sweden, Norway and Denmark – are rather precarious, while 'strong' government has been displayed in Finland and Iceland.

ISSUES AND CHOICES

What political and economic issues do the Nordic countries face in the Northern Flank? There have been a number that have covered the region as a whole and which have affected the Nordic states' influence capability and stress sensitivity.

One phenomenon seen in Northern Waters over the past ten years has been the extension of countries' maritime domains out to 200 nm or to median lines. This has created a patchwork of economic and fisheries' zones on the map of the North Atlantic, in the northern part of which the Nordic states are dominant.[31] Norway has by far the largest sector, one which envelops not only its mainland but also Svalbard and Jan Mayen. Denmark has to protect fisheries' zones around Greenland and the Faeroes as well as its part of the North Sea, and Iceland was the first country in the area to enforce a 200-mile fisheries' limit. These countries have also laid claim to the relevant parts of the continental shelf off their lands, and some are busy exploring and exploiting petroleum resources therein.

There are a number of consequences of this territorialization of the high seas by the Nordic states in Northern Waters. First, it has provided extra resources – mainly in the form of fish and oil – for these countries, but ones which are susceptible to world market conditions. Whilst this development may allow the governments involved greater international influence through access to these products, it also makes their societies more sensitive to stress created by being part of a wider world market – for instance, for petroleum.

Second, the Nordic countries have been involved in a number of demarcation disputes over their continental shelves and fisheries'/economic zones. Many of these have been between traditional allies – those between the United Kingdom and Iceland (the 'Cod Wars') being the most famous. There have been others that have been solved either by bilateral agreement (Denmark–Sweden in the Baltic) or by conciliation (Norway–Iceland over Jan Mayen) or that remain to be agreed (Norway–Iceland–Denmark concerning Jan Mayen–Iceland–Greenland). The most noticeable dispute between potential enemies is that over the delineation of the maritime frontier between Norway and the Soviet Union in the Barents Sea – some 155 000 km^2.[32]

Third, because of their increased economic, legal and political involvement in Northern Waters, the Nordic peoples – especially those in Iceland and Norway – have perhaps been made more aware of strategic activities in the North Atlantic, in particular the Soviet maritime presence. This has made it easier for the Norwegian and Icelandic governments to take a more robust attitude towards defence questions and has perhaps made the Home Rule governments in the Faeroes and Greenland more circumspect when dealing with security issues. Indeed, it can be argued that awareness of the Soviet military presence – in Northern Waters, in the Kola Peninsula and in the Baltic – has led opinion in Norway, Denmark and Iceland to become more supportive of NATO membership than ever before. In 1984, a record 67 per cent of those questioned in a Norwegian opinion poll thought that NATO brought security to their country, and in Denmark polls have shown support for NATO to be over 60 per cent.[33] A survey in Iceland showed that 80 per cent of those stating an opinion (53 per cent of all respondents) were in favour of NATO membership by Iceland.[34]

However, this is only one side of the story. Public opinion in these countries has also shown increasing concern about the perceived 'nuclearization' of Europe and has turned against the Superpowers – the USA as well as the Soviet Union – which are thought to be responsible for this situation.[35]

The response of the Nordic centre-left parties to this concern about (in particular) NATO's Dual Track decision and the Soviet's emplacement of SS20s in Europe has been to turn to the idea of a Nordic Nuclear Weapon-Free Zone (NNFZ). Proposals for a NNFZ have quite a history but until October 1980 they were almost always the preserve of Finnish politicians, especially President Kekkonen. In October 1980, it was Ambassador Jens Evensen – a former cabinet minister in the Norwegian Labour government – who disinterred the notion and followed up by publishing a draft treaty. Further proposals came from President Koivisto, the Norwegian Labour Party and Olof Palme.[36]

The NNFZ proposals have now been integrated into Nordic politics.

They were originally seen by their proponents as a way to increase their countries' influence capability by trying to halt the spread of nuclear weapons in Europe, and to limit the effect on Nordic societies of the proliferation of nuclear weapons elsewhere. The subsequent debate somewhat exposed the idea, implicit in some NNFZ proposals, that the Nordic states could isolate themselves from the rest of Europe on the nuclear issue. The Social Democrat and Labour leaderships in Denmark and Norway insist that plans for a NNFZ can be seen only in the context of wider European agreements, whilst Swedish commentators point to the need for reciprocal action by the USSR in those areas of the Soviet Union bordering the Nordic region.[37] Discussions about a NNFZ are now going through the Nordic mill. Political parties have made their comments;[38] and official parliamentarians and ministers have discussed the issue;[39] and official reports have been issued.[40]

It is perhaps most likely that the NNFZ idea is in for the 'talk at it and tuck it away' treatment. Essentially this is what Nordic politicians did to proposals for a Nordic Defence Union in 1948, plans for a Nordic free trade area in the 1950s and a treaty to establish a Nordic Customs Union in the 1960s. In all cases, a vast verbal expenditure was made with no government being willing to be the first to halt the proceedings, for fear of being damned by their colleagues and their public. Only when alternative options in a wider context became available for some Nordic states – NATO, EFTA and the EC respectively – were Nordic discussions brought to an unconsummated conclusion.

The NNFZ proposals can come to a conclusion in one of two ways. Either they will be overtaken by, say, an INF and/or MBFR agreement or they will be promoted by sympathetic parties coming to power in all the Nordic states. Such parties know that the area is as nuclear-free as possible and that no NNFZ treaty will make it more so, let alone improve the region's security. But this will not stop them from making some sort of joint declaration which may pay domestic political dividends.

The Norwegian Labour Party – in government from May 1986 – has always stressed the importance of seeing a NNFZ in a wider European security context. The Party has also been looking to the rest of Europe in another context. In the referendum of 1972, the Norwegian people rejected full membership of the European Communities and in 1973 a trade agreement was signed between the EC and Norway. Whilst this allowed for consultations on other matters, it fell short of the close relationship with the EC wanted by some Norwegian politicians, noticeably those in the Conservative and Labour parties. As disenchantment with President Reagan's policies has grown, the Norwegian Labour Party has looked increasingly to Western Europe in foreign policy matters. In security affairs it has had discussions with other European socialist parties – especially those in Denmark and the Benelux[41] – and Labour spokesmen have favoured a closer relationship with the Western European Union (WEU).[42] The most difficult foreign policy question facing the Norwegians in the coming decade will be that of their relationship with the EC. Many of the pressures that kept Norway out are not so strong now, and general foreign and security policy considerations suggest a closer alignment with the EC. Whether this can be done without considering formal membership remains to be seen.

When examining the political choices on security issues available to the Nordic NATO states' governments, it should be accepted that the political support does not exist for the sort of demands coming out of Washington or Brussels – substantially increased defence expenditure, support for all aspects of British and American nuclear policies, support for SDI. That these countries *do* have such strong defences for such small populations, *do* have such popular support for NATO and *are* integrated into the NATO Command structure is a tribute to their politicians and people, as well as to the stupidity of previous Soviet leadership. In the face of what many in these countries regard as American stupidity, their politicians may look at the NNFZ option, but this will not give those countries any greater influence capability in strategic affairs, neither will it lessen their stress sensitivity. What might help is the continuation of constructive and often critical diplomacy by these governments in the various bilateral and multilateral talks in which they are involved – in NATO, EC, CSCE, UN etc. Such diplomacy may not bear much fruit immediately, but it certainly has the political support of a wide spectrum of Nordic opinion.

Notes

1. See Chapter 3 by Holst in this volume.
2. The density of population of the Nordic states (excluding the Faeroes and Greenland) is 18 people per km^2 (1983) figure compared with 164 for the

EC, 25 for the USA and 320 for Japan (*Yearbook of Nordic Statistics 1984*), p. 26.
3. For a discussion of this question see Raimo Väyrynen, 'On the Definition and measurement of Small Power Status', *Cooperation and Conflict*, 6, 1971: 91–102; Niels Amstrup, 'The Perennial Problem of Small States', *Cooperation and Conflict*, 11, 1976: 163–82.
4. See, in particular, Peter Hansen, 'Adaptive Behavior of Small States: The Case of Denmark, and the European Community', *Saga International Yearbook of Foreign Policy Studies*, 2, 1974: 143–74.
5. Hansen, 'Adaptive Behaviour': 150. For a discussion of these concepts see Nikolaj Petersen, 'Adaptation as a Framework of the Analysis of Foreign Policy Behavior', *Cooperation and Conflict*, 12, 4, 1977: 221–250.
6. *Yearbook of Nordic Statistics 1984*, p. 27.
7. *Yearbook of Nordic Statistics 1984*, p. 26.
8. *Yearbook of Nordic Statistics 1984*, pp. 82–3; 260.
9. The export percentage going to the USSR is: 1982, 26.7; 1983, 26.1; 1984, 19.0; 1985, 21.5. The important percentage is: 1982, 24.6; 1983, 25.7; 1984, 23.1; 1985, 21.0.
10. This was seen in the rise of the Progress Party in Denmark and Norway in the 1970s and the neo-liberalism of conservative parties in Norway, Denmark, Finland and Sweden.
11. *Nordisk Kontakt*, 1986, 3: 10; 12.
12. Toivo Miljan, *The Reluctant Europeans* (London: Hurst, 1977) Chapters 4, 5 and 6.
13. In the past, Finland came under Swedish and then Russian rule but managed to maintain its culture and separate identity. Norway was part of the Danish kingdom and then a joint kingdom with the Swedish monarchy. Iceland was a Danish colony but got home rule early this century. None of these states was subjected in the way that the Balkan states were under the Ottoman Empire.
14. Krister Wahlbäck, 'The Nordic Region in Twentieth-Century European Politics' in Bengt Sundelius (ed.), *Foreign Policies of Northern Europe* (Boulder, Co.: Westview Press, 1982) pp. 9–10.
15. Barbara Haskel, *The Scandinavian Option*, (Oslo: Universitetsforlaget, 1976) p. 19.
16. Krzysztof Drzewicki, 'The Conception of Administrative organs in the Nordic Council of Ministers', *IRAS* 1980, 4: 343–53.
17. Victor Pestoff, *Voluntary Associations and Nordic Party Systems* (Stockholm: University of Stockholm, 1977).
18. *Working Together? An Opinion Poll of the Nordic Countries Spring 1983* (Copenhagen: AIM and the Nordic Council, 1983).
19. Lars Rudebeck, 'Nordic Policies Towards the Third World', *Nordisk Kontakt*, 1986, 3.
20. Paul Villaume (ed.), *Fredshåndbogen* (Copenhagen: RN-forebundet, 1983) Chapters 8 and 9.
21. *Tredje Parlamentariska Forsvarskommittens Betänkande* (Helsinki, 1981).
22. *Nordisk Kontakt*, 1985, 4.
23. Excluding John Lyng who had 30 days in office in the summer of 1963.

24. H. C. Erlandsen, I. Glomstein and E. Moen, *Fra Solidarisk Sikkerhetspolitikk-til Uklarhet og Unnfallenhet* (Oslo, 1985).
25. *Nordisk Kontakt*, 1986, 3: 47.
26. *Schultz Sortebog. Forsvarslove 1982* (Copenhagen: Schultz, 1982); *Politisk Revy*, 460, 5/84.
27. Clive Archer, *Greenland and the Atlantic Alliance*, Centrepiece 7, Summer 1985 (Aberdeen: Centre for Defence Studies) pp. 10–22.
28. Archer, *Greenland* pp. 11–20.
29. Archer, *Greenland* pp. 22–39.
30. *Utanrikismal Skyrsla Geirs Hallgrimssonar utanrikisradherra til Alpingis 1985* (Reykjavik, March 1985) pp. 26–34.
31. Clive Archer and David Scriviner, 'Frozen Frontiers and Resource Wrangles', *International Affairs*, 59, Winter 1982–3: 59–76; Willy Østreng, 'Delimitation arrangements in Arctic seas: Cases of precedence or securing of strategic/economic interests?', *Marine Policy*, 10, 2, April 1986: 132–54.
32. See Archer and Scriviner, 'Frozen Frontiers': 69–72 and Østreng 'Delimitation arrangements': 133–7.
33. Marit Ytreeide and Eilert Struksnes (eds), *Norsk Utenrikspolitisk Årbok 1984* (Oslo: NUPI, 1985) p. 418; Christian Thune (ed.), *Dansk Udenrigspolitisk Årbog 1983* (Copenhagen: DUPI and Jurist-og Økonomforbundets Forlag, 1984) pp. 427–8.
34. Olafur Th. Hardarson, *Icelandic Attitudes Towards Security and Foreign Affairs* (Reykjavik: Icelandic Commission on Security and International Affairs, 1985) p. 9.
35. Jens Evensen, 'Refleksjoner omkring Atomvåben og atomvåpenfrie soner i Europa', in T. Eckhoff and S. Owe (eds), *Nordisk atomvåpenfri sone* (Oslo: Aschehoug, 1983) p. 28; *Danmarks sikkerhedspolitiske situation i 1980 'erne* (Copenhagen, 1984) p. 45.
36. Clive Archer, *Deterrence and Reassurance in Northern Europe*, Centrepiece 6, Winter 1984 (Aberdeen: Centre for Defence Studies) p. 63.
37. Archer, *Deterrence and Reassurance*, pp. 39–47.
38. *Nordisk Kontakt*, 1985, 4: 301, 13: 913: 1986, 2: 16, 3: 4, 4: 2.
39. *Nordisk Kontakt*, 1985, 12: 808, 16: 1109–13.
40. The Dyvig Report (1984) dealt *inter alia* with the question in Denmark, and the Colding Report (1985) dealt with it in Norway.
41. Nikolaj Petersen, 'The Scandilux Experiment: Towards a Transnational Social Democratic Security Perspective', *Cooperation and Conflict* 20, 1985: 1–22.
42. *Norinform*, 24, 3 July 1984, p. 1.

2 A Swedish View
Bo Huldt

The previous chapter places the Nordic states in a specific category or setting: these countries are analysed as a buffer between the Superpowers. From an historical perspective, as well as from today's strategic perspective, this is undoubtedly a valid approach. It reflects both the realities of the Nordic multi-layered buffer in the North between the two blocs (the pattern referred to as the 'Nordic balance') and the traditions of Nordic neutrality.[1] Regardless of varying Nordic security orientations today, there remains a strong streak of Nordic 'isolationism' – a genuine desire to stay out of harm's way, to be on the sidelines of the greater goings-on.

This is a characteristic common to all of the Nordic states, and it is certainly very much reflected in the Swedish penchant for seeing Great Power presence in general in the Nordic region *a priori* as a bad thing. The further away the Great Powers, the better from a Swedish point of view. At the same time, there has always been among the Swedish policy-makers and their advisors an acute awareness of the complexities surrounding the European balance of power. For example, when Swedish Foreign Minister Undén in 1960 in the United Nations General Assembly spoke in favour of 'general and complete disarmament', he also strongly emphasized that disarmament policies could not be carried out in such a way that the balance of power would be destabilized.

Geography creates certain difficulties – the Soviet Union is quite obviously a neighbouring Superpower that can hardly be wished away – and geopolitics have also imposed well-known limitations upon traditional Nordic neutrality, but memories of happier (and not so happy) days undoubtedly linger both with the Nordic neutrals and their Allied sisters. Elements of this are clearly present in the debates over the Nordic non-nuclear zone (NNFZ).

This way of thinking is usually identified with standard small state behaviour and the small state perspective is also justifiably emphasized in the previous chapter. The Nordic states *are* small states. Still, a measure of qualification is called for. The Swedes, for well-known Second World War and other historical reasons, have been far less chastened by their past than have their neighbours and there has also been a marked tendency to view Sweden itself as a small power rather than a small state, a producer not a consumer of security, and this for the Nordic region as a whole. This is the result of an historical accident. Sweden after the Second World War, as a country virtually untouched by the general destruction in Europe, was propelled into an unexpected role as a strong military and economic power in the North, functioning as the supposed 'backbone' of the 'Nordic balance' with its strong air force, large field army, modern arms industry and sometime nuclear threshold status.

Today, and to a growing extent, there also seems an awareness among the Swedes, in contrast to what came out of much of the public debates in the 1970s, that Sweden is a country with a certain and inescapable responsibility for that strategic position between the blocs that destiny has allotted her. There is no way of avoiding this – the message having also been brought home with some emphasis during the early 1980s through various territorial violations. Here one should notice a growing understanding – outside as well as inside expert circles – of the strategic importance not only of the Baltic, a traditional Swedish concern, but also of the North, Norwegian, and Barents Seas for Swedish security.

Comments have been made about the effects of (and also imputed intentions behind) the submarine incidents in Swedish territorial waters. The assumption among some non-Swedish observers of the Nordic scene is apparently that a process of 'conditioning' is going on by which the Swedes are supposed to adjust and adapt to the *real* 'correlation of forces' and the '*poderes facticos*' in the Baltic region.

Even if we were to assume 'intentions to condition', which would be hard to prove, it still seems most doubtful whether any 'adaptation' has taken (or will take) place. Polls taken among the Swedes about the will to resist armed attack, 'even when the outcome appears in doubt', show no real change of heart: The 'same' 80 per cent, who have been believers in the Swedish national defence doctrine since the polls began in 1952, seem as firmly resolved as ever. The only rather drastic change than has taken place since the mid-1970s has been an increase in the Swedish popular view of the Soviet Union as a threat to Sweden and to peace, and this undoubtedly also reflects reactions to the submarine incidents. (Comments about national character are generally a hazardous business and should be avoided, but it *might* be that a particular Swedish touch of 'legalism' will aid the Swedes against presumed 'conditioning'.)

One thing is uncontroversial and that is that the Swedish reaction to the submarine incidents *per se* has been balanced in terms of force posture and defence doctrine. Despite fears in certain quarters on this point there has been no panic away from the balanced defence concept (with priority given to air defence, the JAS-fighter programme, and the modernization of the army) to a new defence structure with a reshuffling in favour of the navy and anti-submarine warfare.

However, there is an indication of a shift of emphasis of a totally different kind. The traditional formula has been that Sweden pursues a non-aligned policy in peacetime, aiming at neutrality in case of war. The new international climate that appeared in the late 1970s which has become known as the 'New Cold War' has been responsible (far more than have submarine intrusions) for greater attention being paid to the importance of non-alignment in peacetime as a policy for stability – rather than as a policy solely preparing for a remote war contingency.

The old formula still stands, but the war scenario cannot claim monopoly on our attention as a guideline for day-to-day policy. Neutrality (or non-alignment) must thus appear at least as much a formula for war prevention, confidence and security-building as for national survival in case of war. The wisdom of this is not new (Swedish politicians of all persuasions have hinted as much since the 1940s), but a new international environment, with *détente* in the 1970s followed by tension and disillusionment in the 1980s, has given it new relevance.

Basically, the Nordic scene and its actors have previously been regarded as a somewhat dull cast. Little action and great stability has characterized the region as seen from the outside world. This fundamental stability has also been associated with the post-war Social Democratic political predominance in the region. A crucial question must be to what extent this particular form of political and social stability within the Nordic states will subsist.

In all of these countries, there presently seems a marked tendency towards the centre, away from political alternatives both right and left. At the same time, it appears that this 'centre' is situated slightly off the 'middle', inclined towards the 'right'. This should be seen as a reaction both to the international pressures upon the region and to growing domestic problems connected with the maintenance of political and social consensus as well as economic difficulties. In the short run, at least, this is an encouraging sign – that consensus and stability (which, after all, has been the key Nordic contribution to the political map of Europe) will be maintained.

This is most obvious in Sweden where the security and foreign policy debate now demonstrates a truly impressive harmony and unity across party boundaries. After the tragic death of Swedish Prime Minister Palme such closing of the ranks is clearly felt to be a necessity for both psychological and political reasons. To some, the 'Palme effect' may seem a short-term factor, that could (for a while) delay very real confrontations between 'right' and 'left' on foreign and security policy. A different view, and the one held by the present author, would be that the 'Palme effect' has combined with a general trend in re-establishing the true consensus on foreign and security issues that has dominated the post-war period but which (temporarily) became a prey to political infighting during the late 1970s and early 1980s.

Also, the trend towards the centre is by no means limited to Sweden – it is also quite apparent in Finland, where the tendency of the 'centre' to move rightwards, away from the 'socialist' alternatives, is most pronounced.

In the long run, things may not necessarily look as encouraging. The present movement towards the centre and away from confrontation could mean that truly difficult issues will be kept submerged in order not to threaten political unity. Depolarization has its costs. One must also observe the tendency towards a fractioned political map with alliances shifting and with 'security majorities' frequently being something quite different from 'social and economic policy majorities'. This is most obviously the case in Denmark, but is also apparent in Norway. But throughout the region there are important shifts from one issue to the other and the electorate in general shows a growing inclination towards mobility and 'unrealiability'. To the extent that this is an indication of the inherited party structure becoming increasingly irrelevant, given the issues rising in highly developed welfare societies, one must view the future with genuine concern. A growing tendency towards confrontational relations – not least in negotiations between unions and employers both in the public and the private sector – may indicate a greater amount of conflict during decades to come even in the North, this haven of orderly and harmonious labour market relations.

Dr Archer in Chapter 1 treats the Nordic states not only as a barrier but also as a group. Even though we may all be aware of the difficulties (and many historical setbacks) of Nordic co-operation over the centuries and recent decades, it is still important to underline Nordic interdependence. The mutual considerations of the interests of the fellow Nordic states have been, and will hopefully remain, important.

To many of us, elements of the Nordic non-nuclear zone (NNFZ) debate has been disturbing, not because of the possible military security complications caused by any possible zone arrangement but because of the centrifugal political effects within the Nordic group. The nuclear-free zone issue has created a measure of dissension in the North, and in 1980–1, when one-time Finnish proposals became first Norwegian, then Nordic and ultimately European issues, the situation appeared rather complicated. Certainly, the public debate may here have created an impression of drama that did not really correspond to the underlying reality. The barrage of political 'persuasion' aimed by advocates of the nuclear-free zone against opponents may have been fireworks rather than substance. It is also worth observing that in the most authoritative statement made on the zone by a Swedish spokesman (Prime Minister Palme's address to the Paasikivi Society in June 1983), it was underlined, with great emphasis, that the issue, like any other security and foreign policy question, would have to be decided upon by each Nordic state in accordance with its own national interests.

Today, we witness what at least appears a more stable state of affairs, with an element of institutionalization of the debate itself and with a general gathering, in this particular case, towards the middle ground. Arguments both for a nuclear-free zone 'at any price' and for outright rejection have become muted. Instead, the present line, since the meeting of the Nordic parliamentarians in Copenhagen on 29–30 November 1985 and the publishing of the Norwegian Colding Report in December 1985, seems to be that the zone concept is interesting and should be pursued, but that there are very considerable difficulties and that further analysis in depth, against a European background, is called for.

Critical commentators have made comparisons between the nuclear free zone and NORDEK, the proposed economic union in the North which 'everybody' supposedly desired but which nonetheless never materialized, for reasons claimed to be beyond the control of the Nordic states. Others have referred to the symbolic implications of the coming 600th anniversary of the once glorious Nordic Union of Kalmar in 1397.

Present analysis of the peace movements have suggested that we may now be in a phase of declining 'nuclear awareness' – although after Chernobyl this would seem a rather dubious proposition. Even if there is presently no strong *popular* pressure in the Nordic countries for the zone, one should certainly not discount the possibility of renewed activism on this issue. However, the factor may work both ways, also suggesting what limited protection a zone might offer.

Regardless of the outcome, whether there will be a zone agreement in 1997, or at any other date, or not at all, a key issue remains to keep the Nordic group and area from disintegrating. Using a naval metaphor, our Nordic 'convoy' in troubled waters, whether escorted or on its own, must not be dispersed. In 1948, Nordic 'unity' to the Swedes meant an Alliance between Denmark, Norway, and Sweden outside the great power blocs. This was not to be, and perhaps this was for the best, but nonetheless there emerged a Nordic sub-system within the wider European framework, and the maintenance of the stability of this system must remain a crucial question to the Swedes (and, we presume, to all our neighbours too).

The basic assumption about the immediate future for the Nordic states – their domestic and foreign policies – must emphasize continuity rather than drama. This certainly applies to Sweden under the new Carlsson administration, and I venture to propose that it will apply to Norway of the new Brundtland administration as well.

An important constraint upon both domestic consensus and defence capabilities is created by the increasingly acute dilemma of 'rising demands and insufficient resources'. This dilemma is certainly not limited to the Nordics alone. It is shown also by the United States' budget deficit; French economic policies and turnabouts during the Mitterrand presidency; and the difficult choices (also in the security sphere) that lie ahead for the United Kingdom in the late 1980s. For the Nordic states, however, as small welfare societies moulded by decades of Social Democratic predominance (although this does not apply to an equal extent to all of them, Finland clearly being a different matter) the dilemma may have a special character. There is in the North an apparent tendency to think of 'welfare' as first, second, and third – only thereafter we may consider other issues. The Aneurin Bevan argument of 1950 – that (over)arming puts intolerable strain upon consensus and therefore threatens the very fabric of the developed, industrial society – has a particular appeal also in the North. In the 1930s, some Swedes referred to the 'fortified poorhouse', when resisting rearmament. The argument is, of course, quite correct, as far as it goes. There is no doubt a point where societal cohesion becomes threatened, and arming against external enemies turns out to be counterproductive because of domestic disintegration.

To establish an optimum balance, however, is the very duty of responsible government.

In Sweden in the 1970s, this way of thinking had a very strong hold on the public debate – and detente in Europe also seemed to provide justification for more relaxed views on security. Today, as I have already indicated, the debate seems more balanced, with realism a much more conspicious component. In Sweden, as in Norway, influential voices have also advocated *increasing* resources for military defense as a response to the Nordic area having become more exposed to the strategic concerns of the Superpowers and the alliances.

Still, one should keep in mind that the 'standard' Swedish (and, presumably, Nordic) reaction to rising tension and force levels – whether strategically, regionally, or locally – is likely to be *both* a call for negotiations and arms control *and* (somewhat less enthusiastically) for increased armaments efforts.

Despite the changes in the climate of opinion on security issues in the North since the 1970s, one should thus maintain a realistic perspective of the possibilities for increased defence efforts among the Nordic countries. For the Swedes, difficult decisions on government spending and priorities have to be faced with the 1987 Defence Plan. For the Norwegians, developments in the international oil market add particular difficulties to keeping up the impressive NATO armaments record since 1977 (and to maintaining societal consensus). There are few indicators that the Danish political system, with its characteristics of extreme minority parliamentary rule, will become more stable. The Nordic periphery – Finland, and Iceland – may today actually demonstrate the most obvious examples of traditional Nordic 'stability'.

'Welfarism', 'detentism', and a balancing act between 'reassurance' and 'deterrence' (or, as is now preferred, 'dissuasion') have been (and are likely to remain) characteristics of the Nordic scene. This all makes for *continuity* – which, however (in the case of Sweden most pronouncedly) also implies a strong national defence coupled with a tendency stubbornly to stand one's own ground.

Note

1. For recent studies in English or in German of Nordic security issues in a strategic, political and economic context, see the References section below.

References

Carl Bildt, 'Sweden and the Soviet Submarines', *Survival*, July–August 1983.
Katarina Brodin, 'Die Nordflanke Europas aus schwedischer Sicht', *Nordeuropa: Ausfalltor des Sowietunion zu den Weltmeeren*; herausg. vom Deutschen Marine Institut (Herford, 1985).
Ingemar Dörfer, 'NATO à la carte', *The Washington Quarterly*, Fall 1985.
J. J. Holst, *Norwegian Foreign Policy in the 1980s* (Oslo: Norwegian University Press, 1985).
Bo Huldt, 'The Strategic North', *The Washington Quarterly*, Summer 1985.
Bo Huldt, 'Public Opinion and Security in the Nuclear Age: The Swedish Case', paper submitted to the 16th International History Congress at Stuttgart (September 1985).
'Nordic Security Today', special issues of *Cooperation and Conflict*, 4, 1982. *Nordic Journal of International Politics*.
Security in the North: Nordic and Superpower Perceptions, (Stockholm: Swedish Institute of International Affairs), Conference Papers 5 1984.
Bengt Sundelius (ed.), *The Neutral Democracies and the New Cold War* (Boulder, Co.: Westview Press, 1986).
Sweden's Security Policy: Entering the 90s, report by the 1984 Defence Committee, SOU 1985: 23 (Stockholm, 1985).
William Taylor and Paul Cole (eds), *Nordic Defense: Comparative Decision-Making* (Aldershot, Hants: Lexington Books, 1985).
Heinz Vetschera, 'Neutrality and Defense: Legal Theory and Military Practice in the European Neutrals' Defense Policies', *Defense Analysis*, 1 (1985).

Conference Discussion

There are obvious interactions between the domestic politics of the Nordic countries and the security situation in which they find themselves. Just as the ins and outs of Scandinavian politics influence the policies of Scandinavia's large neighbours and allies, so might the policies of the Superpowers help mould the shape of domestic politics within Scandinavia.

For example it is sometimes suggested that the sheer weight of economic imperatives will oblige Norway and Sweden to seek closer economic ties with the European Communities (EC), possibly to the extent of actually joining it one day. Despite recurrent problems with the Common Agricultural Policy (CAP), it seems to many that the EC is gradually turning into a country, with a common law, traffic regulations and so forth. In recent years the EC has been developing something of a common foreign and security policy, too. How long can Norway and Sweden afford to resist such political and economic pressures and stay out of it?

Of course, Norway has already had a chance to enter the EC, but the Norwegian people decided in the referendum of 1972 to stay out. However there has been a growth of interest in 'European' political issues in Norway over the past several years. Moreover, this debate has not only been going on in the Conservative party (which has always been pro-European) but in the Labour party as well, which was divided over the referendum in 1972. Since that time there has been a weakening in the political power of those forces which were strongly against membership. The possibility of Norway becoming a full member of the European Community in the 1990s certainly cannot be ruled out.

As far as Sweden is concerned, the question of neutrality is an extra complication in the way of joining the EC, especially as it is developing a common foreign policy. On the other hand, if over the next 25 years a Europe develops which is more distinctively independent of the United States, many of the present constraints on Swedish membership would diminish. For, after all, Sweden since the Second World War *was* once willing to join an Alliance – namely, a Nordic defence Alliance in 1948 – but not a Western Alliance including the United States. There is talk in Sweden about a 'return to Europe' in the sense of being more concerned about European political issues close to

Sweden's boundaries. But Sweden could belong to Europe only if it was totally different from how it is now, and no longer determined by the inheritance of Yalta.

For the moment however, membership of the EC is not a political issue, and is not advocated by any political party or pressure group. There are also more mundane questions about whether Sweden has the technology and the resources to prosper in the EC in any case.

This discussion so far has concentrated on the possible effects of political and economic forces outside Scandinavia on the domestic situation in the various Nordic countries. The influence of military pressure clearly also needs to be thought about.

In this connection, the Swedish parliamentary report on the submarine intrusions that have recently taken place in Swedish territorial waters suggested that amongst other possible motivations, the idea of the intruding power (presumably the Soviet Union) might be to acclimatize or habituate Sweden to the facts of superior Soviet power in the region. Swedes might gradually get used to Soviet submarines in their waters, just as they are to seaweed; they may eventually be persuaded that having Soviet submarines in Swedish waters is an unavoidable fact of life, a consequence of the typical way that Great Powers behave, and that small powers can do no other than to resign themselves to this reality. If this should become the general view in Sweden, it could have important implications for Sweden's attitudes to subsequent Soviet actions, so the long-term effects of such pressure on Swedish opinion need to be considered.

However, there is considerable evidence that such intrusions have had a reverse effect to that possibly intended, in that they have strengthened Swedish resolve and determination to resist such pressure. There has been a rather dramatic change in the attitude of the Swedish population towards the Soviet Union since the era of *détente* in the mid-1970s; it has now become rather like it was at the beginning of the Cold War period in the late 1940s and early 1950s. This change has not been exclusively because of the intruding submarines; there are other issues involved, most notably Poland and Afghanistan.

In view of this, it is surprising that submarine intrusions continue to be reported at an astonishing rate. According to some estimates sightings of probable and possible submarines through the summer of 1986 were as high as ever. Possibly the Soviet Union has just made a mistake over what the results of this policy would be, just as it has over the disputed islands to the North of Japan. This may be another case where Soviet execution of policy has defeated Soviet aims.

It also ought to be remembered that Sweden also has a frontier with the Soviet Union, and that that frontier is a maritime one in the Baltic, and that it is a disputed one. The Swedes, like the Norwegians, are now discovering how difficult it is to negotiate with the Soviet Union over disputed sea areas, such as the so-called 'White Zone' between the Swedish island of Gotland and the Soviet coast. In the past couple of years, there have been several incidents in this area.

It is very difficult to see what the long-term effects of all this might be. There is no evidence (at least yet) that the effects of the submarine intrusions and incidents in the White Zone will lead to the kind of long-term conditioning that has been suggested. One of the reasons why this seems unlikely is that the Swedes have a rather legalistic way of looking at things like this which will dissuade them against such accommodations.

Another kind of military pressure might be exerted against Iceland, a Scandinavian country of considerable strategic consequence for the control of the North Atlantic, in an area where the security perceptions of the Soviet Union and the West might well be dramatically different. So far, discussion has tended to concentrate on what might be termed Scandinavia's continental front with East and Central Europe; but how might a threat to Iceland on Scandinavia's maritime flank influence events and perceptions for Norway, Sweden and Denmark?

The Nordic countries would certainly see anything approaching an attack on Iceland as a major conflagration, with dramatic potential effects for the security of the West as a whole, because of its relevance to the protection of Europe's Sea Lines of Communication (SLOCs) and so forth. When NATO was formed, Greenland, Iceland and the Faeroes were seen as vital stepping stones across the Atlantic, and this explains why the United States were so keen to bring Norway and Denmark into the Alliance, and the British tended to try to do the same for Sweden. These countries are not just of interest for Western European security, but are of vital interest to the United States. Whatever happens in Western Europe, these countries are going to be on the front line. Iceland cannot escape its geography, or the increasing Soviet pressure around its shores.

As a maritime country, Iceland is well aware of the Soviet presence in its waters and their response has been to become more sympathetic to membership of NATO, with all that entails for Iceland. There is in fact much more security awareness in Iceland than there used to be.

Part II
Security in Northern Europe

3 The Security Pattern in Northern Europe: A Norwegian View
Johan Jørgen Holst

NORDIC EUROPE: THE DOUBLE PERSPECTIVE

Traditionally, the north-western region of Europe has been viewed as a flank area from the point of view of the central front. Contingencies like a 'Finnmark-grab' or other limited war scenarios dominated security thinking during the 1960s and 1970s. However, during the 1980s the north and the centre increasingly have come to be considered as an integral theatre from the point of view of military planning. Limited war and *fait accompli* scenarios have receded somewhat. Developments in military technology, renewed attention to the problems of trans-Atlantic reinforcements and changed maritime perspectives have led to a more holistic approach.

From the perspective of the central balance of nuclear deterrence the north-western region of Europe provides an important avenue of approach, as well as an arena for forward defence and deployment. With regard to the global naval balance, the area encompasses primary routes of access to blue waters for the Soviet Union, while it contains a forward defence zone for the trans-Atlantic sea lines of communication for the Atlantic Alliance. It is an important zone of deployment for Soviet submarine-based missile systems. A Soviet SSBN bastion strategy would affect American interest in surveillance and interception, hence the security order in northern Europe is linked inextricably with the variable geometry of the East–West military competition.

THE NORDIC SECURITY PATTERN

The Nordic area does not provide a sufficient framework for regional security. It is woven into various dimensions of the East–West military competition. However, in spite of the strategic significance of parts of the region, it has remained on the whole an area of low tension. Each of the Nordic countries has imposed limits on the direct military penetration of the Nordic area by outside powers. The Nordic area does not contain irredentist pressures or aspirations, nor are minorities threatening the social and political framework of the Nordic countries. Co-operation is both extensive and intensive among the Nordic countries in all matters except those of high policy relating to security.[1]

Instead of constituting a Nordic pact, the Nordic states – for a variety of historical, geopolitical and strategic reasons – have chosen different roads to security. However, in charting their course they have taken into account the impact of their choices and dispositions on each other. Their circumstances and range of choice have been and remain different, but over time their chosen policies have crystallized into a coherent pattern of mutual consideration and restraint. Sometimes the term 'Nordic balance'[2] has been used to depict the pattern. The term is in some sense misleading; no balance has been established among the Nordic states, since they are not poised against one another. The Nordic pattern of mutual consideration and restraint applies most particularly to the military penetration of the Nordic area by outside powers; restraint in respect of one set of outside powers may serve as an obstacle to others. But there is no symmetry with respect to external linkages. Norway, Denmark and Iceland are allied with the Western powers in a much more all-embracing and committed manner than Finland is tied to the Soviet Union through its treaty of friendship, co-operation and mutual assistance. The limits of external military engagement in the Nordic area reflect the fact that the Nordic area is overwhelmingly a part of the West.

The Nordic area exhibits a decreasing degree of integration into the connecting tissue of the Western system of security as we move from west to east; the Nordic pattern is woven into the overall security order in Europe. It is a balanced pattern in the sense of constituting a stable arrangement. The rules of engagement are tacitly observed by the outside powers, and carefully monitored by the inside powers. It is broadly understood that significant changes with respect to the external engagements in the security arrangements of any Nordic country would lead to reassessment in the others, as well as to external pressures for compensatory concessions. Hence, interdependence in the field of security shapes the Nordic part of the security order in Europe. The Nordic pattern is a part of that broader order, rather than a self-contained system of checks and balances.

No military balance has been sought by the Nordic states as a basis

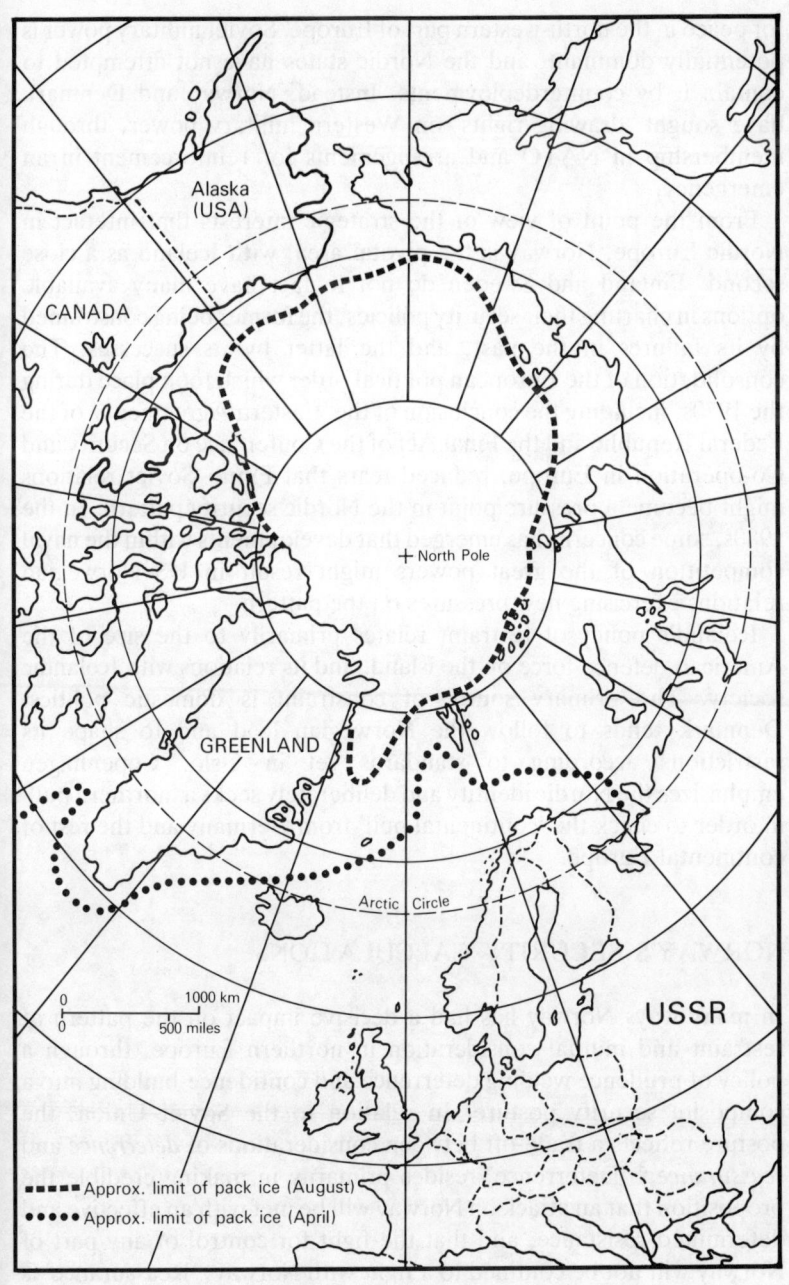

Map 2 Arctic ice lines

for peace in the north-western part of Europe. Soviet military power is potentially dominant, and the Nordic states have not attempted to contain it by counterdeployments. Instead, Norway and Denmark have sought 'drawing rights' on Western military power, through membership in NATO and arrangements for reinforcement in an emergency.

From the point of view of the strategic interests that interact in Nordic Europe, Norway is the pivotal area, with Iceland as a close second. Finland and Sweden do not in fact have many available options in charting their security policies, the former being constrained by its failures in the past, and the latter by its successes. The consolidation of the European political order which took place during the 1970s, including the conclusion of the 'Eastern Agreements' of the Federal Republic and the Final Act of the Conference on Security and Co-operation in Europe, reduced fears that Finno–Soviet relations might become a pressure point in the Nordic security pattern. In the 1980s, some concerns has emerged that developments within the naval competition of the great powers might result in US–Norwegian relations exercising new pressures on the pattern.

Iceland's policy of restraint relates primarily to the size of the American defence force on the island, and its relations with Icelandic society. The primary source of constraint is domestic politics. Denmark tends to follow the Norwegian lead and to shape its restrictions according to standards set in Oslo. Copenhagen emphasizes the Nordic identity and deliberately seeks a 'northern pull' in order to check the 'continental pull' from Germany and the rest of continental Europe.

NORWAY'S SECURITY CALCULATIONS

In many ways Norway has had a decisive impact on the pattern of restraint and mutual consideration in northern Europe, through a policy of prudence welding deterrence and confidence-building into a composite security posture. In relation to the Soviet Union, the posture reflects a trade-off between considerations of *deterrence* and *reassurance*.[3] 'Deterrence' resides primarily in making credible the proposition that an attack on Norway will be met with an effective and determined resistance, and that the fight for control of any part of Norway will not be confined to a fight with Norway. 'Reassurance' is made up of a series of unilateral confidence-building measures designed to communicate peaceful intentions and avoid challenging vital Soviet security interests during peacetime. The policy of not permitting the peacetime stationing of foreign troops, the rejection of stockpiling and deployment of nuclear and chemical weapons as well as the imposition of geographical, quantitative and qualitative constraints on peacetime Allied military activities in Norway constitute the main elements of restraint.

In relation to the United States, the Norwegian posture reflects a trade-off between considerations of *solidarity* and *precaution*. 'Solidarity' involves close co-operation in the pursuit of common ends. 'Precaution' encompasses attempts to prevent allies from pursuing unilateral objectives which are not in tune with Norwegian security interests on the Northern Flank. A policy of precaution would thus attempt to reduce pre-emptive instabilities as well as incentives for horizontal escalation in the north-western area of Europe. Tensions may arise between the global competition of the major powers and regional stability in northern Europe.

Much of the internal discussion in Norway, as well as between Norway and outside powers, has focused on ways of adjudicating competing considerations in relation to specific issues. A policy of prudence involves avoiding the extremes; unmitigated pursuit of deterrence could result in provocation, while maximizing reassurance could lead to appeasement. Automatic solidarity could lead to an abdication of responsibility, and single-minded emphasis on precaution could result in escapism. For Norway there are no easy choices, but still a necessity for choice.

THE CHANGING NAVAL ENVIRONMENT

The post-war pattern of security relations gave the key positions in north-western Europe to the two Nordic states, Norway and Finland, which had no experience or tradition in foreign affairs. Finland experienced the imposition of the logic of the balance of power earlier than Norway, and the quiet Finns seem to have accepted its *diktat* with greater equanimity than the more volatile Norwegians. Tensions between realism and idealism continue to shape the Norwegian debate on security policy.

When Norway, Denmark and Iceland entered NATO as founding members the Soviet Union did not constitute a serious threat to the trans-Atlantic Sea Lines of Communication (SLOCs). However, throughout the 1970s the Soviet naval build-up (which appeared to signal an ambition to contest Western naval supremacy) caused growing concern in Norway, as it tended to cast doubts on the assumption that Allied assistance could be brought to bear on a crisis in order to prevent the outbreak of war, or (in the event of an actual attack) be interposed between the attacker and his objective in Norway.[4] Allied assistance was dependent on transportation by sea, and Soviet submarines and naval aircraft with stand-off weapons emerged as a potent threat against its real effectiveness in an emergency.

It is possible that Soviet naval policy did not in fact focus on threatening the SLOCs, but rather on the task of protecting the strategic missile submarines. A reversal of strategic objectives seems to have taken place in the 1970s; with the first generations of submarine missiles the primary Soviet problem had been to break through NATO's ASW barriers from the North Cape – South Cape exit (between Norway and Spitzbergen) down through the GIUK Gap in order to ensure access to the Atlantic for its strategic naval forces. With increased missile ranges, the Soviet Union could attempt to establish northern 'SSBN bastions', and try to turn the northern seas into a semi-sanctuary by keeping Western naval forces out of the Norwegian Sea. A bonus effect would be, of course, to separate Norway from the sources of planned reinforcements. It is possible also that a 'bastion mentality' could entail increased interests in controlling the littoral states along the bastion waters.

PROVISIONS FOR REINFORCEMENT

In adjusting to the changing geometry of naval power, Norway worked out several arrangements for reinforcement with her primary allies (including prestocking of heavy equipment, spare parts and fuel, as well as the earmarking of forces for reinforcement). The measures involved ground, air and naval forces. However in the specific design of the modalities, particular care was taken to align them with the established pattern of restraint and reassurance *vis-à-vis* neighbouring states. Concerns about peacetime stability had to be weighed against potential efficiency in war. Norwegian authorities were concerned also about not being locked in by inflexible or high-risk defence plans, and about being able to maintain control over the way in which such plans would be carried out in Norway. Furthermore, they wanted to be able to generate repeated responses to ambiguous warning while at the same time maintaining a level of preparedness which makes frequent responses unnecessary.

The Norwegian government decided in 1981 to locate the depots for a US MAB (Marine Amphibious Brigade) in central Norway, rather than in North Norway as had been advocated by the Norwegian military authorities. This siting was designed to emphasize defensive intentions *vis-à-vis* neighbouring countries, as well as to preserve options for flexible response in the event of crisis or war. The option of swinging to the north or the south was thus preserved, and since the concern about not rocking the boat is likely to be strong in an ambiguous crisis, the Norwegian government wanted to preserve the option of calling in reinforcements as a deterrent prior to the outbreak of hostilities without running the risk of precipitating the latter by forward Allied reinforcements. The need to emphasize defensive intentions was strengthened also by the American choice of earmarking Marine Corps units for reinforcement of Norway in view of the accentuation of the offence in its doctrine and posture. The Norwegian government insisted that the MABs air component exclude the long-range nuclear-capable A-6 strike aircraft, and include instead close support fighters. In addition to emphasizing defensive intentions the Norwegian government wanted to secure maximum national control over the conduct of a war in defence of Norwegian territory. The spectrum of flexible options was broadened by the decision to preposition equipment for an additional Norwegian brigade in North Norway.[5]

The United States is the primary Allied underwriter of Norwegian security. However, Norway does not want to transform her need for countervailing guarantees against Soviet military power into the creation of a lopsided client relationship. Her own military efforts constitute also a major protection of sovereignty in the Alliance context. In addition, the involvement of the United Kingdom and the Netherlands (UK/NL LF – United Kingdom/Netherlands Landing Force) and Canada (CAST-BG–Canadian Air/Sea Transportable Brigade Group), as well as the AMF (Allied Mobile Force), provide a multi-lateral framework within which to manage plans and exercises for reinforcement.

The security situation on NATO's Northern Flank should be assessed with reference to possible contingencies in order to explore the implications of structural weaknesses and incentives. As already noted, NATO seemed for many years to focus overwhelmingly on the central front while Norway in the context of the nuclear stalemate concentrated on countering the contingency of a limited attack against the northern regions. The Soviet Union is capable of executing a 'Finnmark-grab' with the forces in being on the Kola Peninsula. However, the military gains would seem quite marginal, and the dangers of escalation very large as long as NATO appears reasonably cohesive. The danger of challenging Western control for marginal gains in regions very close to key areas and installations for the Soviet posture within the central balance of nuclear deterrence and the global naval competition is likely to remain forbidding in the eyes of Soviet decision-makers.

A limited attack against the key areas of North Norway has been plausibly blocked by Norwegian and Allied measures and contingency plans; the Soviet Union does not maintain a D-Day capacity in being for such a contingency on the Kola Peninsula. The ground forces are quite limited when compared to Soviet deployments in other forward areas and the absence of fighter bombers on the Kola Peninsula does not indicate a clear and present danger of limited attack. Fighter bombers could be transferred to the airfields operated by the air-defence forces (PVO-Strany), but little is known about the actual interoperability among the different air forces of the Soviet military establishment. Norway has tried to ensure approximate equivalence between the leadtimes associated with Soviet reinforcements of the Kola Peninsula and reinforcements of North Norway by NATO. The re-equipment of Soviet ground forces with modern infantry combat vehicles, self-propelled artillery and rocket launchers, a significant expansion of the number of transport and attack helicopters as well as the introduction of special purpose forces (Spetsnaz), and an expanded air and amphibious assault capability may indicate increased emphasis on offensive options. However, the forces of the Kola Peninsula seem to enjoy rather low priority in the Soviet force modernization programmes. The main battle tanks are still of quite old vintage (T-54/55). The tactical air force in Leningrad Military District (LEMD) now include modern fighters (like the Fitter and Flogger). However, the numbers available for operations in the North would depend on competing requirements and overall priorities. For Norway, the task is one of maintaining a political posture through alignment which makes it unreasonable for an attacker to assume that a war in North Norway would remain limited. Moscow should not be allowed to allocate large portions of the LEMD forces to the North.

Instead, those forces should be viewed as needed for the protection of Soviet areas closer to the central front.

In the course of the 1970s the fragmented visions which dictated much of the focus on limited war scenarios were thus gradually replaced by more holistic approaches which focused on the synergistic relations between the centre and the north. The credibility of NATO's commitment to defend Norway depended in part on the ability of the Western Alliance to control the process of escalation in Central Europe. Similarly, NATO's ability to control that process depended on the ability of the Western Alliance to defend the trans-Atlantic SLOCs. In that connection, the ability to operate out of Norwegian airfields could prove vital, as could the ability to deny use of those same airfields to a would-be adversary. The size and topography of North Norway would require a would-be attacker to commit fairly large forces, which would then not be available for allocation to the Central Front or the Baltic region. NATO's ability to hold the Central Front is vital therefore also from the point of view of constraining Soviet options for diverting forces to the northern area.

In the context of a broader war in Europe, the north-western theatre of operations (TVD) is thus unlikely to constitute an area of large-scale Soviet offensive operations in the early phases. Such commitments would divert forces away from the decisive battlefields. In the early phase of a major war in Europe, the primary threat against the northern part of the Scandinavian peninsula probably would derive from a Soviet interest in denial, in the elimination of key portions of its military infrastructure, particularly airfields and naval bases. Soviet planners would be concerned about foreclosing the Western option of opening other fronts in order to relieve pressures on the centre and create new room for manoeuvre.

Denmark and southern Norway are linked directly to the Central Front. In the context of a major war on the continent of Europe, airfields in Denmark and southern Norway could be used in order to affect the outcome. Eastern forces are consequently likely to give priority to strikes against Danish and South Norwegian airfields for purposes of denial, to be followed by ground forces moving north through Jutland. The *'Weserübung* scenario' therefore remains relevant to the security situation in northern Europe.

To summarize, from a Norwegian perspective the contingency of a *fait accompli* in North Norway is deterred by forces demarcating the border and under order to resist attack, and the credibility of NATO's guarantees which would be seriously impaired if a piece of real estate belonging to a member of the Alliance were allowed to fall under the control of an aggressor. The contingency of a *limited attack* against the core areas of northern Norway is blocked by Norwegian and Allied plans and preparations threatening an aggressor with the prospects of a drawn-out conflict pregnant with dangers of escalation. The contingency of a *large-scale attack* in the context of a major war in Europe is deterred by NATO's overall ability to counter aggression, and by the capability to confront an adversary with resistance in Norway which would constitute a serious drain of resources away from the decisive area.

THE MANY FACES OF FORWARD MARITIME STRATEGY

The maritime competition in northern waters will influence the shape and form of the security situation in north-western Europe in the years ahead. The Norwegian perspective will be one of protecting the state of low tension and the infrastructure of restraint and confidence-building practices against the ripple effects of intensified competition in northern waters.

It is still unclear whether the Soviet Union has opted for a SSBN bastion strategy as a long-term solution, or what the salient features of the bastion strategy are.[6] The Soviet Union has opted for a large SSBN force; its physical characteristics have followed the American one through four generations of submarines and ballistic missiles. However, the SSBN forces of the two Superpowers differ markedly in their peacetime operation routines. The major portion of the Soviet force is kept in port at all times. It is not very clear why the Russians have opted for large and fast submarines if they intend to protect them by keeping them in local areas instead of relying on concealment in the open ocean. Nor is it really clear that the Russians view their SSBNs as an investment in a withholding strategy for intrawar deterrence, bargaining and war termination; these are Western rather than Soviet concepts and categories. The arrival of highly accurate missiles provides the SSBN force with potent first strike options as well.

The Russians may have encountered operational difficulties in addition to command and control problems in keeping their force on long and distant patrols. The heartland power may also consider it natural to deploy its sea-based 'artillery' close to shore in order better to co-ordinate its employment in war with other forces. As the Soviet overall naval posture and experience mature, the peacetime SSBN patrol pattern may change in the direction of emulating the US open ocean operations.

If we assume that the Russians have indeed opted for a SSBN bastion strategy, the question remains how best to contain the threat it poses to Western interests in general, and American interests in particular. Carrier battlegroups and surface action groups may seem ill-suited to contain and attack SSBNs deployed in defended nearshore bastions. If American SSNs were used for purposes of trailing Soviet SSBNs in their bastions and under the polar ice, they would sail into the dilemma of how to deter Soviet pre-emption while simultaneously placing the Soviet SSBN force at risk. New tensions could be brewing in northern waters which would throw shadows on to the shores of the Nordic states.

Norway is likely to view with concern an American forward maritime strategy[7] which would go beyond surveillance and aim at keeping the Soviet SSBN force at risk through *peacetime trailing*, as such efforts could increase Soviet interests in securing sanctuaries which extended to the littoral states. Concerns about maintaining a survivable deterrent could come to dictate Soviet priorities *vis-à-vis* the Nordic states, and thereby exercise increasing pressure on the Nordic security pattern. In view of the Soviet priority of protecting SSBN bastions, American wartime pressure on the bastions could divert Soviet naval forces away from threatening the SLOCs (including reinforcements to Norway). However, the dangers of pre-emption and inadvertent escalation would constrain the pursuit of such a forward maritime strategy.

A forward maritime strategy which involves *permanent naval presence* in the Norwegian Sea would similarly seem to break with the pattern of mutual restraint which has been observed hitherto and which made the naval competition in the Norwegian Sea systematically different from that in the Mediterranean. A reasonable frequency of presence is desirable, however, in order to emphasize American commitment to the defence of Norway. Here is another area where considerations of deterrence and reassurance have to be orchestrated into a harmonious pattern.

A forward maritime strategy which involves *horizontal escalation* – e.g., if the Soviet Union should attack in an area of American vulnerability, the United States in response would threaten to escalate horizontally by using carrier battle groups to strike at Soviet points of vulnerability on the Kola Peninsula – seems oddly theoretical in the age of nuclear weapons (even in a country which suffered heavily after Lord Nelson's raid on Copenhagen). In the real world of international relations – as opposed to the battle for funding in the US Congress – American decision-makers are likely to discover that attacks on the Kola Peninsula would entail enormous dangers of igniting a Soviet nuclear response against the continental United States. For a small country bordering on the Soviet Union a doctrine of exploiting vulnerabilities in accessible areas as counter-moves may appear to be imbued with rather uncomfortable consequences. The boomerang effects would loom large, and Norwegians are likely to see their interests best served by rhetorical restraint in Washington.

Norwegian attitudes to the US forward maritime strategy may seem overly ambivalent. For a number of years Norway complained about inattention and worried about falling behind the 'maritime frontiers' of the Soviet Northern Fleet while American attention was absorbed by the central front. A regular and substantial schedule of American naval visits and exercises provides needed containment of Soviet naval power which is homeported in north-western Europe; it provides protection against a sphere of influence growing out of the barrels of Soviet naval guns. Major fluctuations in the pattern of American presence could convey inadvertent messages of changed commitments and objectives. Too much attention, like inattention, can breed tension, however. Policy implications are a product of both substance and style, content and presentation. In many ways, Norwegian concerns about the forward maritime strategy are caused by rhetorical excesses rather than action; the strategy has been presented without proper attention to nuance and precision. It comes in rather hortatory and assertive wrappings, too much salty 'can do-ism' produces the effects of a bull in a china shop in the context of the subtleties of the Nordic pattern of mutual restraint and consideration, and the checks and balances of the state of low tension in north-western Europe. America has her own legitimate national interests to protect in relation to the Soviet SSBN force, but the manner in which it is done is important to the Nordic states with their vested interests in stability and low tension.

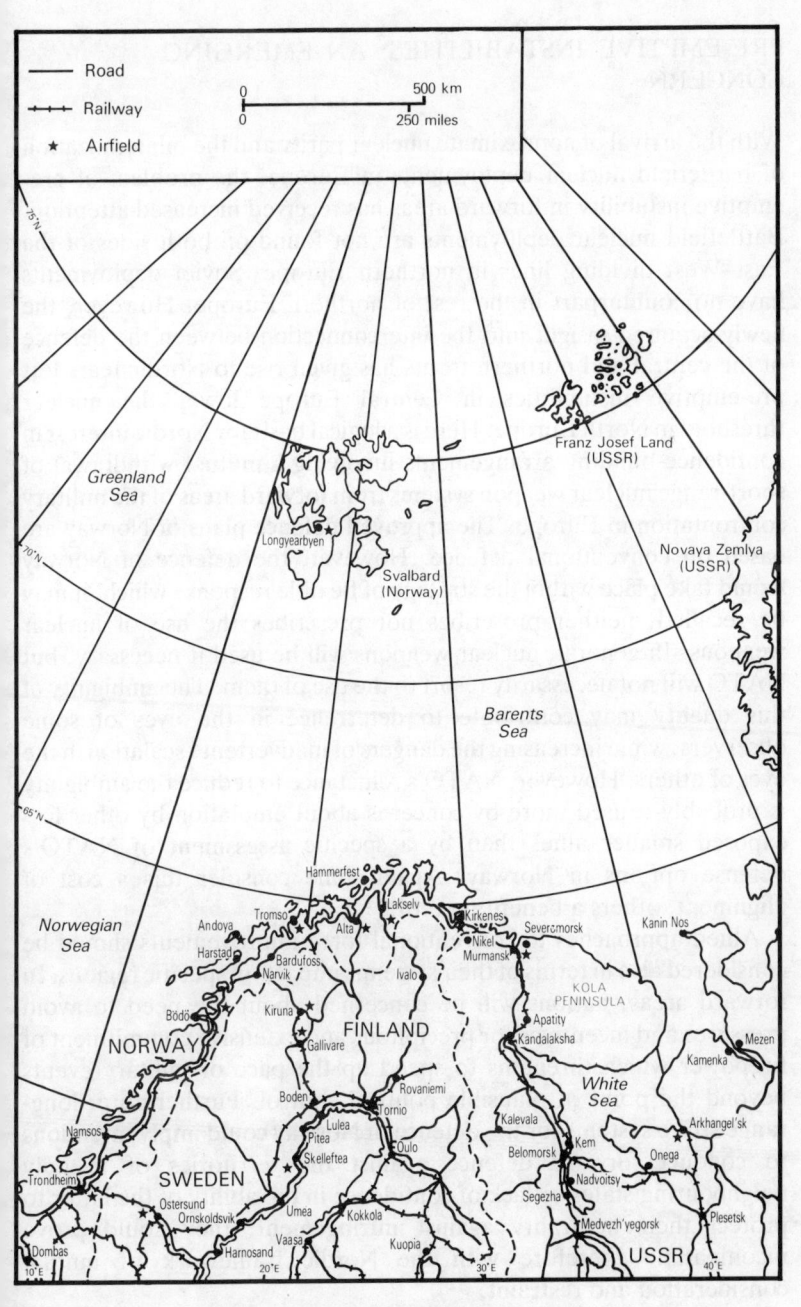

Map 3 Svalbard and the Barents Sea

PRE-EMPTIVE INSTABILITIES: AN EMERGING CONCERN

With the arrival of approximate nuclear parity and the bilateralization of battlefield nuclear deployments in Europe, the problem of pre-emptive instability in forward areas has received increased attention. Battlefield nuclear deployments are not found on both sides of the East–West dividing lines in northern Europe. Soviet deployments have no counterpart in the rest of northern Europe. However, the newly-acquired insight into the interconnection between the defence of the central and northern fronts has given rise to Nordic fears lest pre-emptive instabilities in Central Europe lower the nuclear threshold in North Europe. Here is a logical basis for Nordic interest in confidence-building arrangements involving a mutual withdrawal of short-range nuclear weapon systems from forward areas of the military confrontation in Europe. The approved defence plans of Norway are based on conventional defence. However, the defence of Norway would take place within the strategy of flexible response which, it may be recalled, neither proscribes nor prescribes the use of nuclear weapons. In general, nuclear weapons will be used if necessary, but NATO will not necessarily resort to the use of them. The ambiguity of this duality may contribute to deterrence in the eyes of some observers, while increasing the dangers of inadvertent escalation in the eyes of others. However, NATO's reluctance to reduce the ambiguity is probably caused more by concerns about emulation by other less exposed smaller allies than by a specific assessment of NATO's defense options in Norway. Again some consider this a cost of alignment, others a benefit thereof.

Allied approaches to conventional force improvements should be considered also in terms of their systemic impacts in specific regions. In forward areas, nations will be concerned about the need to avoid pressures and incentives for precipitous and extensive commitment of firepower which threatens to speed up the pace of military events beyond the point of plausible political control. Furthermore, long-range strike systems for the defence of Norway could imply intentions to conduct forward defence against the territories of friendly neighbouring states or lack of confidence in the ability of the latter to protect their neutrality against infringement; they could prove incompatible therefore with the Nordic framework of mutual consideration and restraint.

Traditionally the Soviet Union has invested heavily in early warning and anti-bomber defences on the Kola Peninsula. The arrival of long-range cruise missiles is likely to give a new lease on life to the strategic bomber, and hence to Soviet interests in protection against it.

Both the Soviet Union and the United States are in the process of developing and deploying long-range cruise missiles on ships and aircraft. A competitive build up of sea-launched cruise missiles projects the danger of inadvertent escalation, as well as a lowering of the nuclear threshold – both because of the intermingling of nuclear and conventional versions of the same missile and because of the linkage between naval deployments and options for the conduct of a ground war in Europe provided by ship-based cruise missiles for land attack. Such deployments may also reduce the chances of negotiating an agreement for the reduction of intermediate range nuclear forces capable of hitting targets in Europe. This appearance of an increased nuclear emphasis in the arms competition has stimulated Nordic interests in arrangements which might reduce the ambiguities which could lead to inadvertent nuclear escalation. Re-emergence of the debate about a Nuclear Weapon-Free Zone (NNFZ) in the Nordic area could be viewed also in this context.

NUCLEAR WEAPON-FREE ZONES: THE QUESTION OF FRAMEWORK

The idea of a NNFZ in the Nordic area has evolved through many stages and sponsorships.[8] In the wake of the great nuclear debates of the early 1980s the idea has become an established part of the Nordic security scene. In fact, it has brought security issues into the Nordic Council via conferences of parliamentarians, and may become the subject of joint Nordic studies and investigations on the official level. At the same time, the idea is sufficiently vague to encompass a plethora of competing schemes (and objectives). In fact, it has become the currency through which exchanges about framing conditions for the security policies of the individual Nordic countries takes place. It has caused strains on the Norwegian consensus about security policy, but nevertheless it is broadly agreed that there should be no isolated Nordic arrangement. A NNFZ in the Nordic area would have to be an element in a larger structure of commitments and agreements leading to a reduction of nuclear weapons in Europe in general, and nuclear weapons capable of threatening targets in Nordic Europe in particular. We have thus come full circle. The security arrangements in

Nordic Europe are but a part of the broader East–West balance in Europe. There are no easy escapes, but a need to consider ways of stabilizing the security order in Europe at large.

Notes

1. For further elaboration, see Johan Jørgen Holst, 'The Pattern of Nordic Security', *Daedalus*, 113 (2), Spring 1984: 195–225; Johan Jørgen Holst (ed.), *Five Roads to Nordic Security* (Oslo: Universitetsforlaget, 1973); *Nordic Security Today*, special issue of *Cooperation and Conflict* 17(4), 1982; Erling Bjøl, 'Nordic Security', *Adelphi Papers* (181) (London: International Institute for Strategic Studies, 1983).
2. For an elaboration of the concept, see Arne Olav Brundtland, 'The Nordic Balance and its Possible Relevance for Europe', in Daniel Frei (ed.), *Sicherheit durch Gleichgewicht?* (Zurich: Schulters Polygraphischer Verlag, 1982) pp. 119–38.
3. For further elaboration, see Chapter 5 in Johan Jørgen Holst, Kenneth Hunt and Anders Sjaastad (eds), *Deterrence and Defense in the North* (Oslo: Norwegian University Press, 1985) pp. 93–132, as well as Chapters 2 and 3 in Johan Jørgen Holst og Daniel Heradstveit (red.) *Norsk Utenrikspolitikk* (Oslo: Tano, 1985) pp. 33–76.
4. For background, see Christoph Bertram and Johan Jørgen Holst (eds), *New Strategic Factors in the North Atlantic* (Oslo: Universitetsforlaget, 1977).
5. The issues are put in the context of the overall policy design in Johan Jørgen Holst, 'Norway's Search for a Nordpolitikk', *Foreign Affairs*, 60(1), 1981: 63–81.
6. A very good discussion of the ASW problem is Donald C. Daniel, *Anti-submarine Warfare and Superpower Strategic Stability* (London: Macmillan, for the International Institute for Strategic Studies, 1986).
7. See *The Maritime Strategy*, special section of *US Naval Institute Proceedings*, January 1986, with articles by Admiral James D. Watkins, USN; General P. X. Kelley, USMC and Major Hugh K. O'Donnell, Jr, USMC; and Secretary of the Navy John F. Lehman, Jr.
8. For elaboration see *Spørsmålet om en kjernevåpenfri sone i Norden*, rapport fra et utvalg oppnevnt av Utenriksdepartementet (Oslo: Det Kgl. Utenriksdepartement. 1985); Johan Jørgen Holst, 'A Nuclear Weapon Free Zone in the Nordic Area: Conditions and Options – A Norwegian View', *Bulletin of Peace Proposals*, 14(3) 1983: 227–38; Johan Jørgen Holst, 'En atomvåpenfri sone i nordisk område', Nytt Norsk Tidsskrift, 2(2), 1985: 97–104.

4 The Security Context: A Soviet View
Malcolm Mackintosh

Johan Jørgen Holst has in Chapter 3 raised all the main political, military and international issues involved with clarity, accuracy and thoughtfulness, and I find myself in agreement with what he has said. It is, therefore, not my intention to challenge his views but to look at the problems he discussed from the Soviet point of view. I would like to try my hand at a 'draft' Soviet study of the Northern Flank as it might be prepared for Soviet decision-makers by planners in Moscow responsible for this area in Soviet thinking. It would have been helpful, of course, if we had access to such a study. But in its absence – the normal situation in the Soviet Union – let me try to offer you the views that it might contain.

Such a study would of course start off by presenting the political, historical and geographical factors of the Nordic area as seen from Moscow, where it is assumed to be a number of peninsulas extending into the oceans and seas of the north: the Atlantic and Arctic Oceans and the North and Baltic Seas. The paper would also give a political view of the post-war history of the Scandinavian countries and the North Nordic area from the Soviet viewpoint with two non-aligned countries (Sweden and Finland), and three members of NATO (Norway, Denmark and Iceland). The central military section of the study would, I think, be written in the Ministry of Defence, very much in the style of traditional Soviet general staff presentations: and would be rather compartmentalized and set aside from other types of warfare. Fundamentally, however, this military section would emphasize the view that, in the event of war in Europe, the Soviet Union must ensure that any military advances made in the Nordic area should try to keep up with those in Central Europe – as described by Colonel Jonathan Alford in Chapter 6. I think, incidentally, that this is a strategic concept which might (though without hard evidence) be attributed to Marshal Ogarkov's thinking, when he was Chief of the General Staff. Soviet military planners will say that what must be avoided at all costs is an exposed or inactive Northern Flank on the right of the central axis. I believe that this is a central strategic principle of Soviet military thinking for military operations in the Nordic area.

Before looking at the way in which this principle of avoiding 'operational isolation' in the North might be put into action, let me note that for the Soviet Union, the first military priority in the Nordic area would be to plan (and carry out in the event of war) the optimum employment of the Northern Fleet, in its two operational elements (see Table 4.1). The first of these would be the strategic operations and

Table 4.1 Strength of the Soviet Northern and Baltic Fleets

Type	Northern Fleet	Baltic Fleet
SSBN	40	—
SSB	2	6
SSGN	30	—
SSG	7	6
SSN	45	—
SS	50	20
CV	1	—
CHG	—	—
CGN	2	—
CG	9	1
DDG	17	7
FFG	8	6
CL	2	2
DD	3	5
FF/FFL	45	25
FAC(M)/Missile corvettes	25	50
Light forces	25	115
MCM	65	125
LPD	—	1
LST	8	5
LSM	6	16
Depot repair/Support ships	30	10
Underway repl. ship	7	3
Support tankers	10	5
Hovercraft	5	25

Sources: Jane's Fighting Ships (1986) Soviet Military Power (1986).

protection (where feasible) of its SSBN force, whatever its mission might be – for example, a strategic nuclear strike against the United States or other Western countries. The second element is the surface Battle Fleet and its submarine and air components. The Northern Fleet would participate in a naval confrontation with the United States and other NATO naval forces in the area, and also undertake interdiction of the Sea Lines of Communication (SLOCs) wherever these may be. The Fleet would be required to keep the United States and other Western naval forces as far away from the Kola Peninsula as possible at all times, in wartime or before the conflict began. This element of the Fleet (with the co-operation of ground, air and amphibious forces) might seek bases in Scandinavian coastal areas later in the campaign – e.g., in Northern or Central Norway.

Let me now return to the strategic principle of keeping operations in the north up with the Central Front. Soviet planners would recommend that Soviet naval, air, ground and amphibious forces operating in Scandinavia should move forward in parallel to those in the Central Front. In practice the operation goals of these forces in the north would probably include the western part of the Baltic Sea and the coastal areas attached to them, the Danish Straits and the Danish Islands, the peninsula of Jutland, the North German coast, and possibly southern Sweden, whether or not Sweden was itself involved in war with the Soviet Union. Neutrality would not, in my view, automatically exclude a country from Soviet military use of its territory, its sea coast or its air space, in such a campaign with specific strategic objectives.

The second task of the Soviet forces would be to locate and send forces to deal with the various elements of the ACE mobile forces deployed by NATO to central or northern Norway (see Table 4.2),

Table 4.2   Armed Forces strength: Scandinavian countries

Denmark	*Introduction:* Population of 5 150 000 and in 1985 defense expenditure was $1.007 billion. Armed Forces personnel total 29 600 (with 9900 conscripts) and a reservist strength of 162 200.
	Army: 17 000 (with 8100 conscripts). Standing force 8500. There are 2 divisional headquarters (consisting of 5 mechanized infantry brigades and 6 regimental combat teams), 8 independent infantry battalions and 1 Army Aviation Unit.
	Navy 5700 personnel (1100 conscripts) based at Copenhagen, Korsor and Frederikshavn. Naval forces consist of 4 submarines, 10 frigates, 16 fast attack craft, 27 patrol craft, 13 MCMVs and 8 Lynx helicopters.
	Air Force 6900 personnel (700 conscripts). Tactical Air Command consists of 3 Squadrons of ground attack fighters, 1 Squadron of air defence fighter aircraft, 1 reconnaissance Squadron. The Air Defence Group has 1 SAM battalion and, additionally, there is 1 transport Squadron and 1 SAR Squadron.

Table 4.2   Armed Forces strength: Scandinavian countries – *continued*

Finland *Introduction* Neutral and, through a 38-year-old treaty, committed to repel aggression against herself or against the USSR through Finnish territory. Maintains a permanent UN peacekeeping force providing personnel for UN duties. The population of 4 825 000 spent $725.31 million on defense in 1985. There are 36 500 regulars (approximately two-thirds of these are conscripts). There are also 700 000 reservists (35 000 a year do conscription training, 43 000 do refresher training).

Army 30 900 personnel (22 300 conscripts). There are 7 military areas with 23 military districts. There is 1 armoured brigade, 7 infantry brigades, field and coast artillery, 4 independent anti-aircraft artillery battalions, 2 engineer battalions, 1 signals regiment and 1 signals battalion.

Navy 2700 personnel (just over half are conscripts) based at Helsinki and Turku. Ships consist of 2 corvettes, 12 fast attack craft, 6 patrol craft, 17 MCMV, 3 support ships and 25 landing craft.

Air Force 2900 personnel (1300 of these are conscripts). There are 3 air defense districts. There are 3 fighter Squadrons, 6 operation conversion units, 1 reconnaissance Squadron and 1 transport Squadron.

Norway *Introduction* One of the founding signatories of the NATO Alliance in 1949, Norway has the smallest population of all the Scandinavian countries with 4 150 000 people. Norway spent a total of $1.598 billion on defense in 1985. The total Armed Forces strength is 37 000 regulars (23 200 conscripts). Additionally there are 201 000 reservists.

Army 20 000 (13 000 of this total are conscripts). There are 2 operational, 5 regional and 16 operational territorial commands. Manpower forms 1 brigade, 1 all-arms group, 2 border garrison battalions, an infantry battalion as well as independent armoured Squadrons and artillery regiments.

Navy 7600 including 1000 coast artillery (5000 conscripts). Personnel based at Horten, Haakonsvern, Ramsund and Olasvern (Tromso). Naval forces consist of 14 submarines, 5 frigates, 2 corvettes, 38 fast attack craft, 2 MCMV, 5 amphibious craft, 23 support ships and 1 helicopter Squadron consisting of 6 Lynx aircraft for SAR/reconnaissance duties.

Air Force 9400 (5200 conscripts). There are 5 Squadrons of ground attack fighter aircraft, 1 Squadron of maritime reconnaissance aircraft, 2 transport Squadrons, SAR helo Squadron. For air defense purposes, there are 4 artillery battalions and 1 SAM battalion.

Table 4.2 Armed Forces strength: Scandinavian countries – *continued*

Sweden	*Introduction* Adopting a neutral stance, Sweden has a permanent peacekeeping organization and provides personnel for UN duties. With a population of 8 343 000 Sweden spent $2.784 billion on her defense budget in 1985. The total strength of regular Armed Forces is 65 650 (with 48 900 of this total being conscripts).
	Army 47 000 personnel (including 38 000 conscripts) are based at 6 military commands. On mobilization, there would be 700 000 personnel enlisted (including 100 000 Home Guard). There are 4 armoured brigades, one mechanized brigade, 19 infantry brigades, 60 independent armoured infantry, artillery and anti-aircraft artillery battalions, 1 army aviation battalion (consisting of 4 companies with 40 helicopters).
	Navy 9650 personnel, including coast artillery. Two-thirds of this total are conscripts. Naval bases at Musko, Harnosand, Karlskrona and Gotesburg – the latter existing for support purposes only. Naval forces consist of 13 submarines, 1 destroyer, 30 fast attack craft, 33 patrol craft, 31 minelayers, 34 MCMV, 147 amphibious craft, 6 icebreakers. There are 2 helicopter Squadrons (comprising a total of 10 aircraft). The coastal artillery consists of 5 brigades.
	Air Force 9000 personnel (just over half are conscripts). There are 524 combat aircraft looking after 4 air defense districts. Squadrons include 6 fighter ground attack, 12 air defense, 6 reconnaissance, 1 transport and 1 operational Conversion Unit.

Source: *The Military Balance* (1985–6).

once hostilities had begun. Possibly this might involve a ground operation through Finland so as to reach as quickly as possible the ACE deployment areas over the Norwegian frontier, but here again this is a very speculative judgement. If such an operation took place, there is no doubt in my mind that the Finnish forces (and indeed any Swedish forces which were involved) would put up very stiff resistance. The third priority is Northern Norway itself. I agree with Johan Jørgen Holst that there is no evidence of Soviet planning for an imminent occupation of Finnmark by strong forces at an early stage in the war. The Russians could, of course, use their forces to seize radar sites and other installations on the Norwegian coastline. Such forces might try to occupy certain fjords to give crippled vessels of the surface fleet facilities for repair. These, I believe, would be the major tasks allocated to Soviet forces currently stationed in the Far North in the event of war.

If this proves to be, in general terms, the Soviet war plan for the North, what is likely to be the Russians' peacetime approach to it? On a very personal basis, I believe that the Russians continue to insist on proclaiming Soviet 'ownership' of the Baltic Sea, as the Superpower with an extensive Baltic coastline. This I think is one of the main explanations of Soviet naval activities in the Baltic Sea over the last ten or twenty years, which also has very deep traditions in Russian history. There is, incidentally, a similar Soviet attitude to the Black Sea, again a semi-closed sea as far as the Soviet Union is concerned. I can't help recalling that in the early part of this century the Russian Empire signed a treaty with the Persian Empire, in which the Persian Empire gave up ownership of the whole of the surface water of the Caspian Sea to the Russian Empire. This treaty, as far as I know, has not been denounced by the Soviet government. Indeed one can see a certain amount of activity in the Caspian Sea in support of this claim. Soviet Naval vessels belonging to the Caspian Sea flotilla exploit this treaty when they transit the most southerly areas of the Caspian Sea, along the Iranian coast. So I do believe that Soviet Naval forces in the Baltic Sea operate in accordance with this general principle, and try to demonstrate a kind of Soviet ownership of the Baltic Sea.

Second I think that there is a Soviet desire to try to limit defence co-operation among the Nordic nations and to avoid, if possible, improvements in co-operation or consultations between the Nordic countries on defence issues. The Soviet Union will also hope to exacerbate any quarrels or differences there may be between the Nordic members of NATO and other members of the Alliance, particularly the United States. They will, for example, lay great stress on criticism of United States Naval strategy for the northern part of the North Sea, and the Arctic Ocean. Moscow would like to keep the United States and non-Nordic members of NATO out of the Nordic area politically, militarily and in other ways. Third, as Johan Jørgen Holst has mentioned in Chapter 3, there are the nuclear-free zone (NNFZ) proposals for the Nordic area emanating originally from the former President of Finland, Urho Kekkonen. These proposals are, of course, strongly supported by the Soviet Union, which tries to build up more Nordic and other Western political support for them. Fourth I think the Soviet Union hopes to relate its existing European arms control offers to Nordic issues wherever possible. For example, the Russians constantly stress the problem of the flight-paths of western cruise missiles through Nordic air-space. In addition to these policies, the Soviet Union will always try to present the Soviet Union as the 'natural friend' of Scandinavia today, and in the future. This is very much part of the Soviet propaganda contribution to their overall strategy for the Nordic countries.

Whether or not this speculative presentation of a hypothetical Soviet document prepared for the Politburo is approximately correct, I do believe that the governments and public opinion in Nordic countries are very aware of the Soviet threat and the nature of the Soviet aims, strategy and tactics in the North. This understanding can be seen in a large number of high-calibre articles and press commentaries, in discussions which we have with Nordic figures, and in a great deal of Nordic diplomacy towards the Soviet Union.

Conference Discussion

Military power and the potential to carry out certain activities in wartime have considerable effects on the situation in peacetime. For example, there are several reasons which would make it difficult for the Soviet Union to encircle Norway from the south and from the north, even assuming Soviet leaders would wish to. Operationally, the task would be difficult and would require so many forces that it would be difficult for them to do the other things that such a scenario would make necessary, and this would be a strong deterrent. More to the point, two of the countries in question – Norway and Denmark – are strongly attached to the NATO Alliance and so much more would be at stake than the fate of two particular Scandinavian countries. Such linkages may well be necessary to preserve the stability of the region.

On the other hand, there is the danger than a strong deterrent posture may be construed as provocative by the other side. The Forward Operations concept recently enunciated by Admiral Watkins (US Navy) might be just the case in point. We should not get so wrapped up in detailed operational discussions about warfighting roles that we forget what the political and deterrent consequences of all of this might be.

In this connection, a sensible and coherent attitude towards maritime arms control might have a real contribution to make to deterrence and stability in this area, perhaps by providing a certain amount of reassurance to the Soviet Union, rather than simply feeding their paranoia. Perhaps it would be worth exploring maritime Confidence-Building Measures in this area? Such an endeavour might, so to speak, socialize the Soviet Union into more constructive attitudes towards the West.

As to what these Confidence-Building Measures might be, the Norwegians have expressed an interest in the idea of prior notification of major naval exercises, though the major maritime powers have been less happy with it because it conflicts with notions about the freedom of the seas. There has also been discussion about the idea of formally undertaking not to maintain permanent naval forces in the Barents and Norwegian Seas, so that the area will be, so to speak, demilitarized. Abstinence from the peacetime trailing of SSBNs seems more far-fetched because it is difficult to verify.

The trouble with such arrangements as these is that in the context of the Stockholm negotiations, at least, arrangements would have to be generalized, and it does not follow that what would work in the North would necessarily work in the South or the Centre. The way (say) that Norwegians and Rumanians feel about force levels in border areas is not the same as that felt by the Germans because their strategic situation is different. We may have to loosen up the generalized system that was created in Helsinki and try to differentiate more, tailoring the arrangements more to the specific requirements of each area.

Another example of this kind of problem is to do with amphibious forces, which the Norwegians are for obvious reasons very sensitive about. But as soon as negotiators seek to create symmetrical arrangements which apply to the Americans as well as to the Russians, they get into trouble. The Americans operate from much further away, and it would be much more difficult for them to provide notification of impending amphibious manoeuvres at the time of embarkation than it would for the Soviet Union. To make progress, we will have to get away from the simple world of the peace researchers where everything is neat, simple and geographically symmetrical.

On the other hand, a policy which seeks to prevent war by providing reassurance to the Soviet Union could have dangers, too. For example, a deliberate policy of not maintaining strong maritime forces in the Norwegian Sea might amount to handing it over to the Soviet Union, which would have all sorts of unfortunate strategic and political consequences for Norway and the other Nordic countries. From the Norwegian point of view, it is absolutely necessary that the Americans continue to pay attention to Northern waters; it is important that there is a fairly stable American presence there so that NATO does not inadvertently send messages that might lead the Soviet Union to suppose it thinks the North of declining importance, or accepts that it now has a lower capability to affect things in that area.

Moreover, Norwegians have to accept that they cannot dictate what the US Navy does in this region, because the Americans have their own, legitimate reasons for being there. Soviet forces in the area could constitute a direct threat to the United States. But the Norwegians, like their local allies, could be much affected by what the US Navy does up there possibly for its own purposes; indeed various ways of coping with an evolving situation of threat in this region could quite likely have quite different results for the various participants and bystanders. For both these reasons, there is a need for a permanent and constructive dialogue between the Europeans and the Americans about maritime policy in this area. There has in this respect to be a balance between national and collective interest.

The same kind of arguments can be applied to the Baltic, which the Soviet Union has for years tried to turn into a kind of closed sea, free from the forces of other nations outside it. In the 1924 Conference of Maritime Disarmament in Rome, the Soviet Union proposed a reduction in their naval tonnage from 400 000 to 280 000 if the other nations agreed that no outside naval forces should enter the Baltic. This shows how important is historical continuity to Soviet perspectives.

Only in the Russian language is there a real phrase which means 'maritime frontier', and they apply this to various seas which they think ought to be contained within it. The Baltic is one such place; and it also applied to the Black Sea where NATO naval vessels sailing legitimately about are always strenuously objected to. In 1946, the Soviet Union tried to rewrite the Montreux Convention to make this possible, seeking to bilateralize it into a treaty between a large, powerful and victorious Soviet Union and the much weaker Turkey. The same kind of thinking is exemplified in the Sea of Okhotsk in the Far East, where American and other naval vessels are deeply resented. In a sense this reflects the Soviet Union's continental land power traditions.

Interestingly, though, there have been some slight signs of movement in the Arctic. A few years ago Soviet demands in the Arctic seemed to imply substantial claims over air and sea space in that area, but they have to an extent retreated on this. Although in Soviet domestic legislation many of the seas to the North are described as historic seas or internal waters, the base lines they have claimed in the Arctic and the Sea of Okhotsk are just about in accordance with the UNCLOS Convention. Perhaps this movement on the Arctic (and indeed their policy at UNCLOS as a whole) is a consequence of the growth of their air and sea power and of the expansion of their distant-water fishing fleet. No doubt the Soviet Union would like to have their cake, and eat it too – by closing their seas but at the same time preserving their access to other people's.

For this reason, it is important for the West to insure themselves against the danger that all these areas will become part of the Soviet Union's maritime frontier. This traditional and evidently strong Soviet attitude of mind goes a long way to explaining why they behave the way they do in the Baltic.

This also explains why Germany wants to keep more than two

Western flags flying in the Baltic. Other countries coming in to show the flag and conduct exercises will help prevent the Baltic from becoming a kind of *mare sovieticum*. We must make sure that the same kind of thing does not happen as did in the northern part of the Norwegian Sea during the Soviet exercise Summerex 85, when there were only a few NATO naval forces in the area ready to react appropriately to whatever the Soviet Navy did.

It is certainly true, in connection with both the Barents and the Baltic Seas, that in their endeavour to manage their security environment Soviet leaders try to construct political relationships with other countries in which they have the upper hand. As long as they confine the Baltic to the littoral states, that is what they will have, because this device would exclude the only naval powers which can contain the Soviet Union.

The same thing takes place in the North, where they try to bilateralize relations with Norway by saying that these are all joint concerns. They know very well that in military strength (and in most other relevant indicators as well) the Soviet side of this condominium is much stronger than the Norwegian, and so will naturally tend to dominate the way things are settled. That is why in Norway it is seen so important to stress that relations in the North should be seen as just part of general East–West relations. In other words, Norway wants the situation in the North to be 'multi-lateralized'.

As a last point, it is perhaps worth speculating that the Soviet Union is not only trying to consolidate its own maritime frontier, but also to penetrate other people's, at first economically and then militarily. Although it is far outside the bounds of the subject being addressed in this book, one of the most interesting apparent examples of their trying to do this is in the South West Pacific which they have for years regarded as being within the maritime frontier of the United States. Perhaps the same could be said about Soviet activity in the Caribbean?

Part III
Britain and the North

5 An Overview of British Defence Policy in the North
Admiral Sir William Staveley, GCB, ADC, First Sea Lord

Before we concentrate on Northern issues, it is right and proper that I should conduct a brief *tour d'horizon* of the global scene so that the Northern Flank is seen in perspective. Today, the United States and the Soviet Union dominate (and will continue to dominate) the world political stage, as the Superpower representatives of opposing political ideologies. It would seem to be no coincidence that the Soviet Union has developed – and continues to enhance – a global maritime capability which supports their political aspiration wherever and whenever 'opportunity knocks'. The Soviets, while ever mindful of the security of their homeland and the importance of their strategic rocket, land and air forces, are alive to the possibilities of sea power, and have probably made greater advances in their maritime capability than in any other military (or non-military) area.

The United States has reacted with the development of their own global military strategy, with a firm maritime base and commitment to a capable '600 ship navy'. For them, in what they have described as an era of 'violent peace', a manifest ability to win a global war is the critical element in preventing one, with peacetime operations and response in time of crisis being crucial contributions to maintaining stability. In economic terms we should remember too, that in 1985, the United States traded more with Japan than with Western Europe. The strategic impact of the Western Pacific littoral states, a cauldron of economic activity and potential growth, must not be underestimated. That the United States looks to their West as well as to their East must thus be recognized, as well as the fact that the Soviet Pacific Fleet is more or less the equal of their vast Northern Fleet, which is so much closer to our European homelands. My message here is clear: while we should not doubt the United States' commitment to the security of Europe and her contribution to NATO, we must recognize two points:

1. It is the European nations' fundamental duty – and indeed the prime responsibility of all governments – to provide an equitable, balanced and credible contribution to their own security.
2. We in Europe cannot neglect the possibility of United States' 'draw down', or 'draw west', in the context of their global commitments and strategy: this reinforces the imperative that the European nations provide significant forces for the defense of their own moat.

Beyond the NATO area, bounded geographically and somewhat arbitrarily by the Tropic of Cancer, we all (not least the United Kingdom) have national interests, which demand our attention and play a part in the shaping of our military forces. While this important component of our strategy must never be forgotten – and our recent history emphasizes the need to be able to react to the unexpected almost anywhere – it is our contribution to NATO which remains the foundation of our country's security policy.

Within NATO Britain provides powerful naval forces to each of the three major NATO Commanders – SACLANT, SACEUR and CINCHAN (see Table 5.1). NATO does not differentiate between

Table 5.1   Ships of the Royal Navy: strength as at 1 April 1986

Serial	Type/Class	No.
1	**Submarines**	
	Polaris	3
	Fleet	13
	Oberon Class	9
	Porpoise Class	2
2	**ASW carriers**	3
3	**Assault ships**	1
4	**Guided missile destroyers**	
	County	2
	Type 82	1
	Type 42	10
5	**Frigates**	
	Type 22	8
	Type 21	5
	Leander Class	19
	Rothesay Class	2
	Navigation training ship	1
6	**Offshore patrol**	
	Castle Class	2
	Island Class	7

Table 5.1 Ships of the Royal Navy: strength as at 1 April 1986 – *continued*

Serial	Type/Class	No.
7	**MCMVs**	
	Minesweepers	7
	River Class	12
	Minehunters Ton Class	13
	Hunt Class	10
8	**Patrol craft**	
	Bird Class	4
	Coastal training craft	15
	Peacock Class	5
	Falkland Islands patrol vessels	3
	Gibraltar search and rescue craft	2
9	**Support ships**	
	Submarine tender	1
	MCM support ship	1
	Seabed operations vessel	1
10	**Royal Yacht/Hospital ship**	1
11	**Training ships**	
	Fleet tenders	4
12	**Ice patrol ship**	1
13	**Survey ships**	8

Source: *Statement on Defence Estimates 1986* (London: HMSO, 1986) pp. 69–70.

maritime and continental strategies: any idea that these two concepts appear to be discrete is illusory and wrong: they are in fact complementary. Our troops and Air Force in Germany demonstrate commitment to the forward defence and reinforcement of mainland Europe, and are therefore part of the forward defence of Britain itself. And in the Northern region our maritime and reinforcement forces are committed to its defence as well. They too are an integral part of the forward defence of our islands: collectively, we must be able to demonstrate the will and capability to sustain the reinforcement and resupply of our islands, the central European mainland and the flanks such that we cannot be isolated from the United States. If we were to surrender sea control to the Soviet Union, we would stare defeat in the face through strangulation of our supply lines. Our Armies and Air

Forces in Europe would wilt and succumb – and sooner rather than later. The complementary nature of the land and maritime campaigns is indisputable, and nowhere is this more clearly demonstrable than in the Northern Flank area. NATO's ability to maintain an effective deterrent posture in this crucial (and usually climatically inhospitable) region in peace and tension requires a most carefully orchestrated balance of capable forces. These forces must be seen to train and exercise where they would have to fight, with the unequivocal support of the NATO countries most concerned.

Consider the situation if we were to relax our guard in this strategically important area, putting at risk the sparsely populated region of North Norway, then Iceland and the Faeroes and thus placing the North Sea and the United Kingdom so much closer to the front line of Soviet forces, needlessly exposing ourselves to a greater threat which would make warfighting a much more daunting prospect for NATO. Put another way, if we were to permit the Soviet Navy free reign north of the Greenland–Iceland–Norway Gap, their front line would be closer to this country than the inner German border: that is a prospect which I would not relish. And such a 'latter day' Maginot Line concept at sea would leak like the sieve that it is: the access of Soviet naval forces (and in particular their submarines) to the Atlantic would be much less easy to interdict should hostilities occur. We should be aware how much geography does not favour the Soviet Northern or Baltic fleets, and we must exploit this constraint to our advantage. We should also be mindful of the fact that the Norwegian Sea is bounded on all sides (save for the Arctic itself) by NATO territory, and any suggestion that the Norwegian Sea be allowed to become a '*mare sovieticum*' must be strongly resisted. Quite the reverse must be our aim, and we should seek to achieve in any future conflict as much sea control as we require to support the reinforcement of this exposed flank and the integrity of all NATO territory, no matter how remote or sparsely populated. And that means a regular presence and a bank of experience in those areas in peacetime. Right now.

Recognizing the vital importance of the Northern Flank to the conduct of maritime operations in the Norwegian Sea and Atlantic as well as to the defence of the United Kingdom itself, we commit substantial resources to the defence of the region.

The UK/Netherlands Amphibious Force (UK/NL AF) would be ready early in a time of tension to reinforce Norway or the Baltic approaches. The UK provides all the shipping, with its integral command control and communications facilities, for this force. 3

Commando Brigade Royal Marines, reinforced by the 1st Amphibious Combat Group and an independent company of The Royal Netherlands Marine Corps, provides a landing force of approximately 6500 men, 2000 vehicles, 10 000 tonnes of stores and 40 of its own organic helicopters. This force, with its own airborne mobility, is self-sustaining and can deploy overtly or covertly, poise or withdraw as the situation demands, land and redeploy as necessary. A range of options for providing a future amphibious capability, once the existing ships come to the end of their planned life, is being carefully studied now, and the way ahead should soon be much more clear.

In addition to this UK/NL AF, we contribute strongly to the *ACE Mobile Force* for which Britain provides Jaguar aircraft and about one-third of the troops and the *UK Mobile Force* – consisting of a British infantry brigade, with its own logistic and helicopter support.

Having mentioned the UK's amphibious, land and air contributions, I will now turn, in a little more detail, to the maritime scene.

I must make it clear, straight away, that the defence of Norway and control of the Norwegian Sea are inseparable; they are indivisible parts of what must be seen as a sub-strategy for the entire Northern region, which must itself form a coherent part of NATO's overall strategy. Having said that, I hope you can see that the importance of the Norwegian Sea campaign must not be underestimated. Soviet domination of the NATO territory-bounded area would enable them to fulfil their maritime objectives more easily. If their increasingly capable submarine-based Northern Fleet can be contained by NATO forces and attacked in depth through the judicious forward deployment of our submarines, ships and aircraft, then I believe we should be able to deny the Soviets their objectives while achieving our own. Our goal must be to achieve the timely arrival of reinforcement and resupply shipping, not just across the Atlantic but to discharge their sustaining cargoes safely in whichever European port it is required. All of this will require the most careful integration of NATO's many and varied maritime assets. Demonstration in peacetime of our capability to achieve the maritime element of this strategy is fundamental to deterrence, and our aim must be to convince the Soviet Union of our solidarity and determination that this strategy would succeed.

At this point, it is pertinent to take a closer look at the environment of the Norwegian Sea theatre of operations. It is all too easy to forget the harshness of Northern waters and the unusual geography of the Norwegian littoral. For what such statistics are worth, Norway's coastline length – if stretched out – is longer than the whole of the eastern seaboard of the USA. The use of Norway's fjords and leads and offshore islands for a range of maritime and amphibious operations, as well as a protected reinforcement route from South to North, merits special attention in its own right. Inshore anti-submarine warfare, and the use of the topography to support air defence and the conduct of air operations and tactical mining all come to mind. Study of the seabed reveals much about submarine operation possibilities. The marginal ice zone, and constant movement of the ice line itself, play their part in complicating the scenario, and the dark world under the polar ice brings a new and challenging dimension to anti-submarine warfare. On the surface, extremes from summer heat and perhaps calm seas and fog to bitter cold and gales in the long dark winter, call for robust, capable ships. Above all, men trained to operate effectively in this kaleidoscope of climatic and environmental variety are essential. Peacetime exercises and deployments to practice all that we may have to undertake in war must be an important component of our deterrent strategy. Ready and capable forces must demonstrate the weight we attach to the maritime security of the Northern Flank.

Our nuclear-powered hunter-killer submarines, and those of the United States, are the platforms best able to operate well forward and threaten the whole range of Soviet submarines and high-value surface units. Good surveillance is paramount, and space, airborne, surface and sub-surface sensors all play an important part here. The deployment of reinforcement forces must be timely, and accompanied by sufficient maritime supporting elements to ensure their safe arrival and sustainability in-theatre. The nature of maritime warfare is such that its inherent flexibility does not permit the painting of one scenario. If we dared to choose one by preference, the very nature of conflict – which requires us to expect the unexpected – would dictate that a quite different scenario would prevail. Keeping the initiative is perhaps the most important operational tenet, and the insertion of carrier battle groups, additional amphibious forces and other surface units into the Norwegian Sea to carry the fight to the enemy must remain flexible in terms of timing, scale and precise mission. The options must be carefully thought through and rehearsed as necessary. I emphasize, however, that it is a simple matter of speed, time and distance which dictates that NATO's European Navies will be in the arena early in a time of tension, ahead of the major US Navy contribution. European maritime forces must be able to hold this area and apply credible deterrence right now in peacetime, as well as in a period of rising tension.

I am well aware that the implementation of forward maritime defence in waters to the North of the United Kingdom cannot be achieved easily, or overnight, in terms of ensuring that we are properly equipped for the task. I do believe, however, that it is dangerous folly to turn our backs on such a strategy. On the question of relative strengths at sea it is difficult to draw an accurate balance, but if – for the sake of debate – we deduce a broad equivalence of NATO and Soviet orders of battle, it is worth restating a point which my predecessor, Admiral Fieldhouse, has made on many occasions. Whereas on land the classical formula of a three-to-one advantage may be needed to launch a successful offensive, the same is not true at sea where the raider (the Soviet missile-firing submarine is an example) can wreak havoc even if outnumbered, just like a terrorist or guerilla. That our maritime forces are able to compete, on these terms, in Northern waters would clearly be to our advantage.

So far, I have – as you might expect – leaned towards the maritime component of defence of the Northern Flank and I justify this not simply because I am privileged to be professional head of the Royal Navy, but because the development of the Soviet Navy over the last two decades may perhaps be recognized, by future historians, as the most significant change of the post-Second World War era. While the arms control debate, embracing the high-profile strategic defence initiatives (SDI), is to be encouraged, and could lead to agreement on a reduction of the number of offensive systems, it is abundantly clear that the Soviet Navy will not itself be subject to any dismantling. Why do the Soviets need such vast fleets, far beyond the requirement for defence of their homeland, upon which NATO has no territorial design? One must deduce that they understand the value of sea power and the influence they may bring to bear through its carefully considered, global application. That the United States is pledged to a 600-ship Navy by 1990 is to be welcomed, and European navies too must play a full part in providing sufficient maritime forces to counter the Soviet threat, not least in Northern waters.

I have referred to the United Kingdom's commitment to providing reinforcement forces to Northern Flank areas, and I do not intend to address land and land-related air operations in any depth: other distinguished speakers will do so. However, it would be remiss of me if I did not emphasize the importance of the airfields in North Norway, both to the maritime and land campaigns. Their use by NATO's aircraft requires no emphasis. Similarly their denial to Soviet use is paramount so that the latter's strategic reach to the south cannot be extended. North Norway's proximity to the huge Soviet military arsenal in the Kola Peninsula is all too apparent from a glance at the map, and we should look to how best, from a military viewpoint, we might square up to this vast military complex. Turning South, to the more temperate but still strategically important Baltic Approaches, Denmark and the Schleswig-Holstein area, we must be ever alert to Soviet ambitions here as well. The Skaggerak and Kattegat must be 'corked up', should hostilities occur, to prevent Soviet egress from the Baltic, and security of this whole region which links the Northern Flank and Central region deserves our full attention.

Through the collective strength of the NATO Alliance, we in the West have enjoyed the longest period of peace in Europe this century, and it must be our aim to perpetuate this state of affairs so that we may foster our cherished democratic way of life and the aspirations and prosperity of all our people. To achieve this, as the years go by, will present a range of difficulties. Given a proper understanding of the nature of the threat, and the will of nations to invest in collective deterrence, we shall succeed. Small or large, populous or not, each nation must look carefully to the percentage of its GDP which should be devoted to its security needs. Look at it this way: what is certain is that no nation doubts its responsibility to provide the best possible social security to its people, and spend a good slice of its GDP accordingly. To quote a recent top politician, surely peace with freedom is the most important social security of all to provide. The Northern region has many unique characteristics and the Nordic states are particularly aware of their own pattern of security. I understand the sensitivity of the 'Nordic balance' and the Finnish and Swedish position, which must be accounted for and respected. Within NATO, there will continue to be debate (bilaterally and in the NATO forum) over issues such as the level of pre-positioned war stocks, permanent stationing of the forces of one NATO country in another, the intensity and frequency of exercises in peacetime, reinforcements plans and command and control: this debate is healthy and necessary. What is important at the end of the day is that agreement on these and other matters is satisfactorily achieved, that the Alliance's collective posture and cohesion are maintained and that burden-sharing among member nations is perceived as fair and reasonable.

My overview would be incomplete without touching on the

possibilities which new technology offers in the context of the Northern Flank's security. The exploitation of space extends the maritime horizon, and offers improved communications, navigation, surveillance and targeting possibilities. In conjunction with the development of longer-range, stand-off weapons, the project of power ashore from air, surface and sub-surface platforms assumes renewed maritime significance. The campaign area appears to shrink in size as new sensor and weapon capabilities are developed and deployed by both sides, thus enhancing the prospects for effective forward defence, at the same time making it all the more important to be able to hold back (through forward defence) the improved reach of a potential aggressor. The rapid and secure transmission of data in large quantities, and accurate position finding and targeting, will also play their part in modern warfare: but we should not underestimate either the potential for countermeasures. Complete reliance on satellite communications would, for example, be dangerous. The Norwegian Sea environment provides plenty of scope for deception, evading detection and covert operations (particularly under water and under ice) which must be exploited fully.

In conclusion, it is worth emphasizing that NATO's Northern Flank plays a very important part in British Defence policy thinking: the resources we contribute to security of this strategically crucial region are considerable. The detail of our strategy, based on forward defence, is under regular review, and discussion with all our allies is positive and beneficial to the achievement of a coherent approach. The maritime and land/air components of Northern Flank security are inseparable, and all NATO countries involved in the security of this crucial region must continue to provide the necessary deterrent posture, at all levels. If I have one particular message to impart, it is this: no one should be under any doubt about the United Kingdom's determination to contribute substantially to the continued security of NATO's Northern Flank, through forward defence, and that we wish to achieve this in concert with all our allies.

6 A Change in British Priorities?
Jonathan Alford

THE CURRENT MILITARY POSITION IN THE NORTHERN FLANK

You learn rather early in life as a military officer that virtually every conventional military problem has a left, centre and right. It is a natural way to think about a problem which is basically set by an axis and the terrain and, to make a rather superficial point, it is a way of thinking determined by the human experience and physiognomy. If you have a principal strategic direction, as we seem to in Europe, then there will be something to the left of it and something to the right of it. Because we recognize that the principal and decisive strategic direction in the theatre is one which will be determined by an adversary and not by NATO (a defensive Alliance has no real choice in the matter), and because that adversary is principally a land power, and because the proximate Soviet objective in war at least is likely to be expulsion of American power from the continent of Europe and the enforced political domination of the Eurasian land mass by the Soviet Union, I see no question but that the big arrow is one which drives, as so often in history, across the northern plains of Central Europe.

But even if one surrenders the strategic initiative to the Soviet Union, thus permitting them to determine the decisive region, and the principal axis of attack (which is more or less geopolitically determined anyway), there will be small arrows as well as one big arrow. Thrusts have flanks; flanks create vulnerabilities; flanks must be protected, attended to. However, more than that, flanking operations which are clearly subsidiary in importance to the main strategic direction can nevertheless draw off part of the defence, divert attention, ease the progress of the main thrust in various ways. Furthermore we now have to consider several technologically – driven 'non-classical' factors. I refer, of course, to strategic nuclear forces whose conservation at least will be critically important for any nation which has them – and whose location and relative importance may be determined by quite different factors from those which might be presumed to set up the principal strategic direction (or directions) of a conventional war in the European theatre.

All this is pretty much a preambular way of saying that NATO's Northern Flank cannot be – ought not to become – the principal focus of our strategic thinking and it is for me to make the case that it nevertheless matters that in the allocation of Alliance resources it has a certain irreducible priority. I shall make the case on four principal grounds.

DOES THE NORTHERN FRONT MATTER?

First, that there is a close connection between the Northern Flank and the Central Front in the purely mechanistic military sense that conventional success on that Flank would have a rather direct impact on the fortunes of Warsaw Pact and NATO in the decisive central theatre of operations. I could not say the same for the Southern Flank.

Second, that there *is* a maritime dimension to strategy which, at the least, will affect the ability of the Western Alliance to transfer resources across the Atlantic to hold the centre (and the Flanks).

Third, that shifts in the composition, characteristics and relative importance of strategic nuclear forces have, quite independently of what may happen in the European theatre of war, increased the relative significance of the Soviet North, and especially the Kola Peninsula and Northern waters.

Fourth, and finally, because NATO is far from monolithic the Soviet Union can work some specific threats to member nations by the development of operations via the northern part of Europe which will present acute *national* problems of resource allocation.

I will also be suggesting that the relative importance of the Northern Flank has increased – and not just because the Northern Flank is the theme of this conference: I happen to believe it on technical grounds which I hope to establish. Remember that I still do *not* argue that the North is anything other than a subsidiary theatre to the Central Front. What I am saying is that in a historical perspective there was once some etiolated arrows in the North which all except Norwegians and Danes could more or less afford to ignore; things have happened 'up there' to cause us to thicken the arrows significantly when we draw our strategic maps, that when the Alliance and its member nations have to consider the allocation of resources and attention it has no alternative but to listen to those who argue, as I do, for a somewhat greater claim for the

Northern Flank because the *military* position has changed, and will change further. Clive Archer makes the political case in Chapter 1; I will simply say at this point that I believe that the political context has also changed in ways which make the North more and not less important and so more demanding of our attention.

So let me return to my four principal grounds for claiming that things have changed. The first is the military relationship or connection between the Northern Flank and the Central Front – and let me at once say that I am speaking of the Northern Flank as NATO does, as Allied Forces Northern Europe, from Schleswig-Holstein to Kirkenes on the Soviet border in Finnmark. Simply as flanking operations to operations on the Central Front, the Soviet Union will tend to see Denmark and Southern Norway as distinct from and more important than North Norway – for very obvious reasons. Indeed, there is some evidence that the line which divides the Soviet central strategic direction from the northern runs through *central* Norway. They will be seeking to deny NATO the use of air bases in Denmark and Southern Norway from which to launch attacks against Warsaw Pact forces operating on the Central Front. Beyond that – and clearly at a much later stage – it would be greatly to their advantage to be able to utilize those bases themselves. Second, they will wish to deny NATO the possibility of launching flank attacks Southward through Schleswig-Holstein. And, third, they would like to open the Baltic Straits to permit access to Soviet repair yards in the Leningrad area but this matters only in a rather protracted conventional war.

There is thus a marked *air* emphasis in the first instance, with land and maritime operations secondary to air operations. All this would be much easier if they can keep Sweden neutral. If Sweden's neutrality is violated at an early stage, air operations against Denmark and Southern Norway become much more hazardous. If only in parenthesis, I would thus like to note that much of what the Soviet Union has been doing to Sweden recently is to remind Sweden in no uncertain terms that it would do well not to get involved on NATO's side in a war. We have been seeing a conditioning of Sweden to *stay* neutral in any East–West conflict.

Even a substantial reduction of NATO air defences in Denmark and Southern Norway would open a corridor through which Soviet aircraft would safely pass to turn NATO's central front air defences. But independent air operations may not be enough to take out (and keep out) of action the airfields in Denmark and Southern Norway – and will certainly not permit those airfields to be put to Soviet use. Nor will air operations alone check flanking attacks on Soviet forces moving West on the Central Front. They must thus engage NATO ground forces by amphibious assault and by swinging some grounds forces northwards through Lübeck.

This is where maritime control of the Baltic becomes critical for the Warsaw Pact and why, in my view, a force of West German (and Danish) submarines together with Tornado in the anti-shipping role become critical for NATO denial of Soviet maritime control. Without massive air superiority and a more massive ASW effort in the Baltic than seems possible, the Soviet Union is likely to find both long-range amphibious operations and air-landing operations in Denmark very hazardous. Nor would I like to be the man who had to lead an amphibious force into the Danish archipelago against unsuppressed shore-based missiles and strike aircraft.

So my judgement would be that the Soviet Union has the capacity to prevent NATO from developing a major threat to the flanks of Soviet forces in Central Europe by keeping forces in Denmark and Schleswig-Holstein too busy to do much, but that they cannot be sanguine about turning NATO's flanks in that direction. Pin down rather than knock out must be their immediate objective. They must assume that the Straits will be closed to them by mines which can be cleared only by establishing control over the very narrow waters and the adjacent coasts. That will not be easy, it will take time and require rather large forces to achieve. Contrary perhaps to the conventional wisdom, I believe that the greatest threat comes not from the sea but from large ground forces turning north through Schleswig-Holstein, crossing the Kiel canal and moving through Jutland.

Turning to my second main ground: maritime operations. In part this is about the Soviet interdiction of the trans-Atlantic routes; in part this is about the Soviet need to keep NATO naval forces well away from important Soviet assets; and in part it is about the reinforcement by sea of the NATO north – and all are interconnected. And this is where the focus of attention shifts from the Baltic Approaches to the Far North. I will assert here that it is the Northern Norwegian airfields which are – or ought to be – of greatest concern. I suggest the following syllogism: who controls the Norwegian Sea depends on who controls the North Norwegian airfields; who controls those airfields depends on who gets there first; and who gets there first depends on who controls the Norwegian Sea. I am reluctantly drawn into designing scenarios, and will not go far in this direction because one can easily get lost, but it seems entirely clear that timing is here critical, given that – for all sorts of reasons – neither side can maintain a permanent defensive presence in the region.

General Nathan B. Forrest's neat encapsulation of the principles of war – 'getting there fastest with the mostest' – applies to this region with a vengeance. I must say that I do not see how NATO forces can fight their way into Northern Norway if the Soviet Navy has had time to move out and establish a maritime presence and perimeter with most of the Northern Fleet deployed in depth back from the GIUK–Bergen Gap before the shooting starts. The battle would then be on the line of the Gap but with Northern Norway horribly isolated behind it. Who won that battle on the Gap could very well determine the battle for the Atlantic, and it is not beyond the bounds of possibility that NATO could fight its way back into the Norwegian Sea if it wins the battle for the Gap – but it would then have to do it against unrestricted Soviet land-based air power because the use of North Norwegian airfields would have been lost to NATO. That would be a tough assignment indeed.

But a much more encouraging scenario is the early deployment of NATO naval forces north of the Gap, the reinforcement of Northern Norway before the shooting starts, the transfer of large land-based air forces to Norwegian COBs, and the Soviet Union faced with the somewhat daunting prospect of having to fight its way southwards knowing that it must not leave unprotected the Kola, the SSBNs in the Barents Sea and its own airbases in the Far North.

You must work out your own probabilities, but I am bound to mark the significance of last year's Soviet naval exercises in the Norwegian Sea (in which it certainly looked as if the Soviet Union was preparing to move its maritime barrier further south), and the speed with which the Northern Fleet moved out was rather impressive; and the pattern of the exercise suggested rather clearly that Soviet priorities were to protect the SSBNs, interrupt NATO reinforcements to Northern Norway and to move out to attack the trans-Atlantic reinforcements. What that suggests is that the needs of northern defence come first – and that is not surprising in itself. The Soviet Union has to take seriously two significant threats at the theatre level: one is the offensive capability of American carriers (and I am sure they hear – and pay attention to – the pronouncements of Secretary Lehman and Admiral Watkins on this score); the other is entirely new to them. It is the capability of US attack submarines to strike land targets with conventional or nuclear cruise missiles. The Soviet Union must now try to keep carriers *and* submarines out of strike range. It will not be easy and the threat will, at least in the first instance, keep them on the defensive with little to spare for offensive maritime operations. But – and this point is crucial for the Far North – the *range* of seaborne weapons (whether aircraft or cruise missiles) will pull them into the Norwegian Sea, and they can live there only if they can establish air superiority; and that in turn brings us back to those critical airfields.

It is far more important in the first instance for the Soviet Union to deny those airbases to NATO than to seize them for their own use. If NATO cannot fly aircraft – for ASW, strike or air defence or reconnaissance – out of those bases, the Soviet Union will have gone a long way to winning the battle for the Norwegian Sea. I think the Soviet Union recognizes quite well that operations to secure those airfields by occupation will not be easy. I doubt if they believe that Finland will permit them a free run; I doubt if they believe that amphibious operations in the Arctic are easy against coastal defences and land-based air power; I doubt if they think that an advance through Finnmark towards Tromso is going to be a pushover. But their primary purpose will be served if they can put those airfields out of action and keep them out – whether by air attack, by missile strike or by raiding from the sea or by bombardment.

Moving to my third independent reason for according greater military significance to the North, I will do not much more than reconfirm in this context the technology-driven changes of strategic nuclear postures that seem to me to affect how we look at the Far North. I do not say that the SSBN will become the backbone of Soviet strategic nuclear forces; I doubt that. The USSR will try to solve the growing vulnerability of its land-based missiles forces in other ways, but whether as a strategic reserve force or as an assured destruction force the SSBNs are clearly important to the Soviet Union. Otherwise why invest large and growing fractions of their resources that way? What has changed, of course, is that they have – as it were – 'come home' as a direct result of the very long range of Soviet SLBMs. They thus need not be exposed to Western ASW forces to the same extent, and hence the notion of sanctuaries or bastions close to the Soviet Union of which the Barents (and the Arctic ice cap) is clearly one. That by itself would confer a new strategic significance to the Far North.

But there is more. You need a polar projection to understand that *if* ballistic missile defences were to have significant effect and *if*, in direct consequence, airbreathing systems (cruise missiles and penetrating bombers) were to reassume much greater importance than for the past

25 or so years, the air defences provided from the Kola against US strategic forces assume a quite different role. If I were a long-range Soviet planner, I would worry a lot about the problems of Arctic air defence, and I would link back to the maritime problem by seeing sea-launched cruise missiles on SSNs as a means of defence suppression. The Americans will not publicly come clean on what additional purpose is served by TLAM-N. I think it could have just that purpose of defence suppression. There are two good reasons for according the Far North a strategic nuclear significance that it did not once have. That is another way of saying that it is the Superpower competition which is dragging the reluctant Nordic states into the front line – and that they can do very little about it. Evidence to bolster the case is the creation by the USSR of an *Arctic* TVD to co-ordinate operations at the top of the world.

Finally we come to the assertion that military developments in the Far North cause rather acute *national* problems of resource allocation. I do not intend to say anything about the obvious difficulties in which Norway is placed with its extraordinary logistic, demographic and geographic complexities. That will come in Chapter 9. Nor shall I speak of Sweden's dilemma beyond saying that a strong, armed neutral Sweden is critical for NATO's position and noting that Sweden is finding it increasingly difficult to maintain the credibility of its policy due – primarily – to resource constraints. The Finnish dilemma, generally managed by Finland with almost exquisite subtlety and finesse, is also fascinating but not on my agenda. I shall say something about Denmark because the Danish problem raises in acute form the issue of how much (or how little) a small country needs to do to be assured of external assistance. The Danish assumption – not wholly incorrect, as it turns out – is that the rest of us cannot afford to allow Denmark to be overrun. Thus whatever Denmark does or does not do, others will move. I doubt therefore if Denmark has the option of neutrality, but those of us who commit forces to the defence of Denmark (for our own perfectly understandable national reasons) do expect some minimum of cover from Denmark if we are to expose our forces. The hope, of course, is that by providing assurances of external assistance to Denmark we can somehow stiffen Danish resolve and encourage Denmark to provide a reasonable minimum of defence to cover that reinforcement. The danger, not to put too fine a point on it, is that Denmark will see as removing any possibility of opting out, as ensuring automatic entanglement and destruction. I happen to believe that Denmark, being where it is, has no option. That is its misfortune but Danes do have a remarkable capacity for self-delusion and I see this tension continuing.

However, it is for the United Kingdom that national and Alliance priorities are most in conflict. Although we never say that we are, Britain is at least as much as Flank country as it is Central. Putting that another way, Britain now tends to see the principal threat vector to its own security as much from the north as from the east. In subtle ways, not much advertized, that is already being reflected in resource allocation. The Tornado, in-flight refuelling, airborne early warning, and new ground-based radars are all on account of the new air threat from the North. Historically, Britain has significantly reduced the overall flexibility of its strategic reserve land and air forces in favour of greater dedication to the Northern Flank – and stockpiling there has increased.

In the competing demands on reducing real resources in the next few years, I think we are bound to have increasingly strident arguments within the Ministry of Defence and between London and NATO Brussels about where the priorities should fall. The future of Britain's amphibious forces will, I presume, be the principal focus of these debates but there will in fact be much more at stake than simply two LPDs. Posing the alternatives as a maritime or a continental strategy for Britain falsifies and obscures the issue. Those are *not* the alternatives. Life is no longer that simple. The issue is to define the direction and nature of the principal threats to Britain, and then to reconcile those with Alliance priorities and resource allocation as defined by NATO Brussels. I can say things which officials cannot. If the Alliance is patently failing to satisfy national security needs by setting directions to policy which run counter to deeply-held national convictions of the nature of the threat, Gaullism – to use a kind of shorthand – will flourish.

My principal thesis, in case you have failed to detect it, is that Britain is becoming more of a Flank country as a result of a number of technically-driven developments in the Far North, all of which are having profound and long-term impact on Britain's security. I do not say that we can cut and run from the Central Front, for the political consequences of doing so would be profound, but somehow or other we have to convince our allies in debate that the Far North is *relatively* more important than before (and some, especially Canadians and Americans, recognize this already) and that we need to put together a convincing strategy for handling the gamut of threats from that quarter.

In coded language what I am saying is that my preference for the longer-term, when cuts in capability are again inevitable, is that those cuts shall fall – if they must – on Central Front capabilities and not on capabilities more appropriate for countering the combined-arms threat from the North. I think I know most of the long-war–short-war arguments, and I hear them. Lose the war quickly on the Central Front and there is no long war to fight. In that context, it is argued, navies matter not at all and the Flanks matter not much. I counter that in two ways. First, *perceptions* of weakness on the Flanks can only encourage the Soviet Union to believe that they could turn the Centre if it did show signs of holding; and, second, the Atlantic Bridge must be kept open if NATO is not to lose a longer war even if it were to withstand the first shock. Lastly, there is the never-to-be-forgotten political point that the Alliance cannot choose what it will defend. Forward defence is not a guiding principal only for the Central Front.

Conference Discussion

There is a great deal of uncertainty about the importance placed by the Soviet Union on the North compared to the Centre. On the one hand, there is the argument that the Central Front is where the risks of a general nuclear conflagration are at their highest, and where NATO is best prepared; so this is an area to be avoided if at all possible. Instead an operation just against the North could seem more tempting to Soviet leaders.

But this is not how the Soviet military mind works. There would be terrible tasks in any kind of war, and if they started one deliberately, it would certainly engulf the Central Front as well. Indeed, some would argue that in such a case the Soviet Union would be bound to seek a rapid and decisive conclusion to the war, and the *only* place that that could be done would be on the Central Front.

Attention has tended in recent years to focus on the Far North rather than the Baltic Approaches area, the loss of which would be serious for NATO in general, and Britain in particular since it would open up an air corridor for the attack of the British Isles, and would allow the Soviet Northern and Baltic Fleets to link up strategically. It is the collective responsibility of several NATO states to make sure that this does not happen.

The geography of the Kattegat and Skaggerak tends to be more helpful to NATO than it is to the Soviet Union. It would be very hazardous for the Soviet Baltic Fleet to mount an amphibious assault on the Danish islands in the face of some very capable forces maintained by Denmark and West Germany. German Tornados would be crucial in this role, and so would submarines, and the continuance of the Danish submarine force as well as the German one is to be welcomed.

As far as the defence of Norway is concerned, the experience of the Second World War has a good deal to teach us, though there is danger in paying this too much attention, just as there is in paying it too little. The 1940 Norwegian campaign certainly showed how important it is to have an effective command-and-control system, to consider alternatives and to make the necessary preparations. The fact that we exercise so frequently up there, that we have specialist ships and that we do so much thinking about it suggests that we have learnt the necessary lessons.

Being able to stockpile the necessary equipment in Norway, and being able to conduct more extensive and more adventurous exercises, might be another way of absorbing the lessons of 1940. In fact, there are two sides to the stockpiling question, and one of them would be whether Britain would want to do it anyway. The United States is stockpiling considerable equipment for one of its amphibious forces in Trøndelag. They have to fly in, pick up their equipment, and then go south or north as the case might be. Possibly by the one road (the E6), by air or by sea. Would it be sensible for Britain to put itself in that position beyond the point where it is convenient to have small stocks for exercise and training purposes? Stockpiling so often means that two sets of equipment and ammunition are necessary, rather than just one. If we have only one set we have to have it in a mobile form – in ships that can take it where it will be needed.

In the Second World War, British planning assumptions were several times undermined by the fact that the enemy made use of neutral territory in his attacks. Since the use of Sweden could greatly facilitate a Soviet advance on the Baltic approaches and on the vital airfields of Northern Norway, was this possibility being taken seriously enough? A strong Sweden, prepared and willing to defend itself, could certainly be critical for NATO. A strong Sweden with its tradition or territorial defence means that the Soviet Union would have to allocate significant forces to the suppression of the country, if it wanted to pass over Swedish territory. The Soviet Union does not have massive forces in the area, only two divisions in the Kola and another seven in the Leningrad Military District (LEMD). It is not easy to see what objective would make such an effort against Sweden, with a large proportion of these relatively modest forces, worth their while.

There has already been reference to the possible effects that Soviet submarine intrusions might or might not have on Swedish perceptions and policies (see Chapter 2, pp. 22–3), but it has had an impact on Swedish defence priorities too; there has been something of a reversal in the decline of the provision of ASW forces. The Swedish response has been deliberately to maintain a balanced approach; Sweden has rejected the option of cutting back on the modernization of the army and continues to give high priority to air defence and the new jet fighter, the JAS project. The intention is to avoid a lopsided response, if only because this just might be what the Soviet Union was hoping to produce – though this sounds more than a shade Machiavellian! In fact, over the past decade or so, there has been something of a shift in Swedish defence priorities towards the northern part of the country, and to the need to cope with sudden attacks. The biggest *Viggen* airbase for example is now at Lulea in the North.

Although it is difficult for NATO to say so, the strength of Sweden's neutrality and her capacity to resist are very important. The fact that Sweden is facing the same kind of allocation problems as NATO, only aggravated by traditionally high priorities being given to welfare expenditure, must be a matter of concern.

Perhaps the same considerations would apply to the case of an overland assault on Finland. Getting across Lapland would be difficult and with the memory of the Winter war of 1939-40 behind them the Soviet Union would surely regard this as an operation of high cost, provided the Finns resisted as expected. In some ways the Finnish response to this situation has not been dissimilar to that of Sweden, though in a perhaps more muted way.

On the other hand a Soviet planner might well be tempted to make use of Swedish airspace as a way of attacking the airfields in Northern Norway. Telling Sweden that this was all that was in the Soviet Union's mind, leaving it to them to decide the response, would seem much less risky and costly than a land attack.

In fact, the best way to hold those airfields in Northern Norway would be to get the necessary aircraft in so that air control can be maintained in the area, as far forwards as possible. In addition, there would need to be land forces sufficiently far forward to preserve the airfields against direct or stand-off attack overland. Soviet airpower is not likely to be able to neutralize the Norwegian airfields on its own. Their construction, terrain and approaches make this even more true of the Norwegian airfields that it is of the ones in Denmark.

There is in addition to the prospect of amphibious attack by Soviet forces, air attack or overland attack, the possibility of an attack by one of the Soviet Union's 5 Air Mobile Divisions. But the use of air mobile forces is risky, unless a fairly early link-up with more orthodox forces can be envisaged. Moreover, the Norwegians are making a substantial effort to build up the point defences of those airfields with more guns and improved Hawk air defence missiles; their F-16s can expect to be reinforced by RAF all-weather fighters, US Marine Corps aircraft and so on. Flying the forces in against such unsuppressed air defences as these would be a very hazardous option, and the Soviets might prefer to allocate their air mobile forces elsewhere, such as Denmark or Southern Norway.

Other options might be the use of Spetsnaz forces, or the development of land-based missiles designed for runway denial. That may be the chosen means of ensuring that NATO cannot operate from those airfields in the first instance; it perhaps should not be assumed that NATO can afford to rely on those airfields necessarily being available to take the initial air reinforcements.

In circumstances in which they were, of course, the first priority would be to fly in all-weather aircraft as early as possible. Provided this is done in a timely manner, Finnmark and Northern Norway would be defensible in the context of general hostilities within Europe. With such air reinforcements, the Co-located Operating (Air)Bases (COBs) and the Rapid Reinforcement Plan (RRP), we do have the ability to make things difficult for the Soviet Union in North Norway for a time, even without the sea control that would make seaborne reinforcements possible.

One way of increasing the air component of the defence of Northern Norway, before the carriers come, would be to construct further airfields up there. The Norwegian government has given some thought to this, especially in the area between Trondelag and Bödö. But even the airfields already in place are quite small and not easy to operate from if that use is contested.

Supposing, though, the worst happens, and NATO loses its ability to hold and use those airfields? This raises the prospect for the Soviet Union of not only denying them to NATO but also securing them for their own subsequent use. Rather than risk this happening, NATO would presumably try to blow the airfields up. This would be a difficult undertaking since what is envisaged is not a few craters in the runway, which all experience shows can be rectified quite quickly. A proper professional demolition job of the whole of the operating surface, carried out by Sappers, utilizing devices like demolition chambers built under the runways when they were constructed, would doubtless be necessary.

If it should be that securing command of the Norwegian Sea takes a long time, perhaps because NATO does not have substantial naval forces in place at the outset, then this capacity initially to hold the fort could be quite vital. But there would soon be a need for seaborne reinforcements. And this takes us to the matter of the battle for the Norwegian Sea.

Part IV
The Sea Campaign

7 Maritime–Air Operations in the North: American Perspectives
Robert S. Wood

NATO's plans and exercises for maritime and air operations in the Northern Flank are both rooted in and distinct from a broader set of political assumptions and strategic concepts. The failure to distinguish campaign options in the region from those broader – and prior – assumptions and concepts can only confuse discussion on the intent, dimensions, and flexibility of the campaign now being developed by NATO's Striking Force, Atlantic.

Strategy at its heart is a military plan of action designed to achieve policy objectives and to meet the threats and seize the opportunities identified by policy. Ideally, this military plan of action will not only flow from policy but will be consistent with the diplomatic, economic, and other plans of action also designed to serve policy.

Forces should be raised, organized, and exercised in accord with strategy – that is, force structure and campaigns should reflect both a political judgement and a strategic concept. Campaigns are a connected series of military operations to reach results desired by that judgement and that concept. Campaign plans, in effect, provide the guidance a battle force commander would give his force to reach the strategic objective. As campaign plans are developed and exercised, strategic concepts may in turn be refined or even altered to take into account operational experience. On occasion, even policy presuppositions are modified.

Needless to say, the actual relationship among policy, strategy, and campaign options is never this tidy. Nonetheless, however confused the process, these distinctions are real and are a necessary condition for differentiating the hierarchy of containment policy, the maritime strategy, and the Northern Flank campaign. In assessing plans and exercises for maritime–air operations in the Northern Flank of Europe, it is thus helpful to state the political–military assumptions and the maritime strategic concepts underpinning those operations.

POLICY OBJECTIVES AND ASSUMPTIONS

It is fashionable to cite the rapidly changing political socioeconomic and technological environment, and the consequent necessity for fresh policy choices. Basic geopolitical factors nonetheless change much more slowly. Despite differences in today's culture, technology, and post-colonial developments, the continuity in the configuration of East–West power since the Second World War remains. Should Winston Churchill, Harry Truman, or Joseph Stalin return, they would feel remarkably at home. If the basic issues that divide the Soviets and the Western powers are endlessly fascinating, they seem also fascinatingly endless.

The Soviet Posture

As at the conclusion of the Second World War, so today, the basic interest of the Western Powers is to maintain a favorable balance of power against an authoritarian, continental regime whose imperial control spans Eurasia and is defined by a centralizing ideology and a strong military character. The Soviet Empire retains the traditional Russian concern to counter real or perceived threats by the extension of control on its periphery and by exploitation of the divisions of its enemies. This orientation is reinforced by a Marxist–Leninist cast of mind that is still central both to Soviet risk calculation and to its foreign policy posture. At the core of this perspective is concern that the Communist Party retain unfettered control within the USSR and the Soviet Empire, and that the good of the international proletariat be absolutely identified with the survival and flourishing of the Soviet state.

Operationally, Soviet policy is fundamentally Machiavellian – that is, prepared to use whatever means are necessary to preserve or enlarge the effective power of the state. Soviet strategy is absolutely Clausewitzian – that is, the threat or use of force is conceived as an amoral instrument of policy, determined and controlled in all instances by the political objectives of the state and an accurate assessment of the correlation of forces. Soviet political philosophy is antithetical to any notion of the balance of power, either internally or externally, except as a necessary tactical – if sometimes prolonged – adaptation dictated by necessity (i.e., weakness).

The Soviet approach to warfare follows from the nature of the regime and has been remarkably consistent, even predictable, in the lines of its development. Soviet strategic thought puts great stock on accurately (if possible, quantitatively) assessing the ideological, political, socioeconomic, technical and military correlation of forces. Military planners are acutely sensitive to reducing the range of uncertainty, either in the conduct or the outcome of armed conflict and strive to maintain the highest degree of certitude in command, control, communications, intelligence, geographical distribution of forces and timing. Central to these concerns are an accurate assessment of the correlation of forces, a clearly defined and widely understood military doctrine, and a clear focus on the political objectives of combat. Weapons and technology condition these factors, but are not in themselves absolute. Nuclear weapons are a decisive factor, but in the sense that they necessarily shape the conduct of war and are key indicators of the post-war political position.

The Soviet desire to minimize uncertainty and maximize predictability should not be construed as foreclosing tactical flexibility or fundamental strategic adaptation. Nor indeed should this desire be viewed as at all unique to the Soviet system. It is rather the strength of this desire arising from the historical experience of the Russian state and the assumptions of 'scientific' Marxist–Leninism that gives Soviet military thought its particular flavor. Adventurism, dramatic rolls of the dice, or operations at the margin are not typically characteristic of Soviet behavior.

Following from and consistent with the Soviet Union's basic geopolitical posture, regime characteristics, and military approach, a general line of policy and military strategy has been developed. In simple terms, the grand objectives of the USSR are to exploit the divisions among its enemies and disrupt the unity of the coalition facing it and to minimize the political and military effectiveness of the force that the United States has extended to the periphery of the Soviet Union. In terms of the latter aim, the Soviets seek to maximize their regional conventional superiority on the Eurasian rim, to neutralize the United States's nuclear threat, and to inhibit the United States's ability to control the sea and air space that joins it to allies or to employ the terminus points of sea and air lanes. To the degree that the Soviets can establish the above conditions, their ability increases to create pressure for compliance with their wishes on the part of the surrounding states.

Within the framework of these outlined objectives and conditions, Soviet military strategy ideally aims at neutralizing the Western nuclear threat through fear of a decisive counter- or pre-emptive attack in Europe, Japan, and North America and through the destruction of theater and intermediate range nuclear forces as part of conventional military operations. Indeed, there is today a debate in Soviet political and military circles as to whether they are able to achieve such a position as to reduce the likelihood of nuclear weapons being employed in an East–West conflict. Whether this will be considered possible or not, should the Soviets choose war, they would hope to exploit their regional (especially conventional) superiorities, localize the conflict, and conduct (and quickly conclude) the war on the basis of a rapid, massive movement of forces. These later considerations are especially evident in their approach to Western Europe which still remains the pre-eminent focus of their military attention. Deep air strikes, early establishment of air superiority, rapid ground advance in the center, protection and extension of the flanks – probably accompanied by attempts to so define the goal of battle as to limit Western participation in the defense – these appear to be central components of the Soviet military posture in Europe.

The Western Response

If the central problem of the Western powers since the Second World War has been the maintenance of a favorable balance *vis-à-vis* the Soviet Union, the containment policy flowing from that interest has been characterized by four elements weighted differently across time. The first is the construction and management of a coalition of powers united by a shared strategic consensus concerning the global balance of power, and is at its North Atlantic and European core defined by comparable political values and a high degree of politicomilitary integration. The second element is the conscious and natural establishment of a remarkable degree of economic interdependence based on market trading principles modified by domestic pressures, social concerns, and attempts to accommodate non-Western (some formerly dependent) states to the exigencies of a relatively open commercial order. This economic dimension has at times been accompanied by secularizing and liberalizing pressures. The third aspect of containment has been the transformation of the United States from a non-aligned power, the maintenance and exercise of whose military power across the oceans was largely episodic, into a politically engaged and militarily active Great Power. The critical problem here has been how to project American military power across the oceans, and join it with those of allies in such a way as to reinforce the latter's political confidence while discouraging direct Soviet military pressure. Lastly, the Western powers have sought to stabilize relations with the USSR through nuclear and conventional force agreements, political understandings, and a freer flow of peoples, goods, and ideas across the East–West divide. This attempt at detente, while often characterized as distinct from containment, has in fact been a consistent, if variably weighted, element of Western policy since the early beginnings.

For the purposes of this chapter, the political integrity and military viability of the Western coalition and the joining of US power to that of its allies in a common strategic posture are the crucial elements in the containment policy.

Particularly within NATO the basic assumptions of that policy have included: (i) the integrity and indivisibility of the member states; (ii) the defensive character of the mutual commitment and the emphasis on deterring general war; (iii) the co-operation and (where possible and agreed) the integration of joint and combined forces into a united defense posture; and (iv) the pursuit of technologies and strategies that will husband scarce resources and forestall the militarization of their own societies.

The implication that has been drawn from these goals and assumptions is clear: a forward strategy calculated to reinforce Soviet prudence by maintaining a general correlation of forces favorable to the West and a strategy at once militarily credible and non-provocative of the war it seeks to prevent.

The issue of how to posture forward without precipitating the very war one seeks to forestall is theoretically among the more interesting questions – although I would argue that in practice the military balance is sufficiently non-threatening to the Soviets and the costs of general war are so patently high as to lessen the provocative impact of certain deterrent moves. Nonetheless, the balance of credible threats and reasonable reassurances are the very heart of a deterrent posture.

One fact should, however, be clear – NATO's force posture is intended to deter the Soviet Union, not some abstract enemy or projection of ourselves. That posture must hence play to Soviet sensibilities – i.e., the Soviet conception of risk and deterrence.

NATO's forward strategy thus has the dual aim of preserving the integrity and unified position of all the member states and of posturing in such a way as to deter without provoking war with the Warsaw Pact. In both analyses and war games it is clear that central to Soviet calculations are the cohesiveness of the Western Alliance and the military effectiveness of Western forces and strategy. And, although the threat of escalation from conventional to nuclear warfare and the concomitant link between US ground forces in Europe and the US strategic nuclear force are still the foundation of the Western deterrent, the East–West nuclear balance and the certitude of cosmic destruction in the event of a general nuclear war dictate that a persuasive conventional force posture and strategy be maintained. Should it appear that the West is *unable* to engage in extensive conventional defense, the adversary may believe it is also *unwilling* to engage in either continental or intercontinental nuclear strikes. If a Soviet attack into Western Europe can be halted only by the threat or use of nuclear weapons and is not integrated into a more comprehensive fighting posture, the Soviets, who never make the hard distinction between deterrence and warfighting, can be forgiven for doubting Western resolve. NATO's strategy must thus be based upon both a credible conventional stance and an invulnerable nuclear capacity – both of which reduce the degree of certitude that the Soviets seek on the battlefield and put at risk important Soviet values. It is this perspective that animates the maritime aspects of strategy and the plans for maritime and air operations in the Northern Flank.

THE MARITIME STRATEGY

What has been called in the United States the maritime strategy is not a self-contained employment of naval forces but is a component of a broader national and NATO strategy. In the first instance, as John Hanley and I argued in an earlier article, the strategy is designated 'maritime' rather than 'naval' because 'it is a combined arms strategy, for the maritime theaters, not simply a strategy for the employment of submarines and carrier battleforces'. Combined arms, put simply, means using all of the forces available to the commander in the theater in such a manner that attack on one element of the force exposes the enemy to counter from another element. US and Allied forces will play essential roles in stopping a Soviet thrust into northern Norway and in sinking the Soviet Navy. In budget battles it is relatively easy to partition the threat and decide which platform performs which missions. In global war games, as in war, he who brings to the battle whatever forces are required to achieve superiority generally wins.[1]

Aside from the combined arms aspect of the maritime strategy, there are a number of other critical assumptions to be made. Those assumptions are capsulated by the words 'forward', 'conventional', 'global', 'coalition' and 'deterrent'.

A forward strategy is consistent both with political and military exigencies. In the case of NATO, the political commitment is the mutual defense of the territory of all the member states, and this includes those areas separated by water or non-Alliance countries from the other members – Norway and the Northern islands. Militarily, to maintain the lines of communication between Europe and the United States and to prevent the Warsaw Pact from turning the Northern Flank demands a forward posture. As Vice Admiral H. C. Mustin, Commander Striking Fleet, Atlantic, recently observed: 'The loss of Northern Norway would be a determining factor in the battle of the Atlantic as would the loss of Iceland; the loss of Greenland would be severe; losing control of the Baltic Straits would allow the Soviet Baltic Fleet access to the Norwegian Sea'.

Furthermore, the shortage of maritime forces dictates that those forces be used at decisive places and moments. While many Allied forces are configured for convoy protection in the central Atlantic Ocean, the ability to execute this role depends on the control of Northern Norway. By seizing Northern Norway the Soviets would effectively control the Norwegian Sea, increase substantially the risks in the central Atlantic, and jeopardize the air defense of the United Kingdom and thus degrade Britain's ability to provide air support for the Central Region. Studies indicate that the air battle in North Norway might be decided in the first ten days and the land battle in the first fifteen to thirty days of war. Prudential allocation of resources thus demands that we explore campaign options as far forward as possible.

A forward strategy implies the early movement and deployment of forces. Again the situation in Norway, for example, could require the early emplacement of marines to forestall a Warsaw Pact amphibious assault and the early movement of submarines and carriers to fix and destroy Soviet air and submarine power as far north as possible. The inability to act early and decisively would allow the Soviets to concentrate their force, and would make US support for Europe more problematical.

If the maritime strategy is part and parcel of the national and NATO forward strategy, it is also intended to contribute to conventional deterrence. Naval forces (including most particularly the sea-launched ballistic missile force) continue as as major component of the nuclear deterrent. But, as noted earlier, unless the West maintains a credible ability to defeat the Soviet wartime strategy at both the conventional and nuclear levels, they may well decide under certain circumstances that a perhaps territorially limited but rapid, massive strike in their periphery could lead to successful war termination below the nuclear threshold. The ability to strike important Soviet targets from various points around the Soviet periphery may well affect their calculation to make war or not.

If one looks again at the Soviet political–military perspective, it is clear that (if they believe that circumstances warrant war) the battle should be geographically limited and conducted in such a way as to limit damage to themselves while rapidly overwhelming their adversary. The campaign should be characterized by the highest degree possible of clear control and exact timing. It must be precisely the West's aim to persuade the Soviets that they cannot with any degree of certainty look forward to this desired outcome. Instead they must face a possibly global, protracted conflict in which crucial elements of their military capabilities and political control are put at jeopardy. In other terms, the West must have the ability to reconfigure the terms of the conflict. Conceptually, it should be emphasized this is not entirely new. Those who choose to deter by early reliance on an intercontinental nuclear strike are also in effect threatening global – and cataclysmic – war as the price for a Soviet thrust into the central front of Europe. This capability (and hence threat) remains. Credibility not only at this level but across the board is strongly reinforced if the Soviets understand that they cannot confine the battle to the central front even at the conventional level. A genuine threat in the North and South of Europe and as far away as the Pacific with the prospect of an adversary mobilized for prolonged conflict should strengthen the Western position simply by making it difficult for the Soviets clearly to discern an acceptable war termination position.

It should be patently obvious that such a forward, global, conventional strategy is underpinned by a credible assured nuclear destruction capability. As important, geography, politics and resources dictate that this strategy be both a joint and combined arms effort. It is pre-eminently a design for integrating forces into combined campaigns. And, most crucially, it is a coalition strategy.

A union or a convergence of perspective and planning on the part of NATO and non-NATO states provides the ideal precondition for such a deterrent posture. Peace may never in fact be utterly indivisible from war, but the deterrence of general war with the Soviets may come close.

Obviously those charged with naval responsibility will be sensitive to the attitudes of the states within the maritime areas of operation, and particularly at the so-called 'choke points'. But the fact that even the maritime campaigns cannot be executed solely with naval forces and that the object of our strategy is to complicate Soviet planning across many theaters means that a fundamental understanding among a wide range of states is necessary. The links, for instance, among the European Central Front, the Northern and Southern Flanks, and the Caribbean and Florida Straits should be explicated and understood. Furthermore, the geopolitics of a state that is both European and Asian must be part of our strategic thinking. Political understandings and military co-operation among the states in the Pacific basin may be nearly as important a factor in general deterrence as our defense posture in Europe.

The maritime strategy may hence most fruitfully be viewed as the maritime aspect of a much broader forward strategy – a military posture that flows from the nature of the Soviet threat and the exigencies of the containment policy. The NATO position and the maritime campaigns designed to serve that position are defensive and deterrent in intent. Defense, however, does not require (nor will genuine deterrence allow) a geographically restricted strategy and 'Maginot line' mentality. Whether at the nuclear or the conventional level, the Soviets must understand that their warfighting strategies cannot succeed, and that their political aspirations must necessarily therefore be kept within limits.

In a real sense the maritime aspects of the forward strategy are the most deterrent and the least provocative in nature. It has been noted many times that although war cannot be won at sea, the failure to achieve victory in the maritime theaters could lose the war. This also means that no conventional attack from the sea can in itself be as threatening, for instance, to Soviet control within its own borders and the Warsaw Pact countries as the reinforcement of the Central Front. Soviet naval forces may be destroyed, its bases in Kola and elsewhere may come under attack, its strategic reserves at sea may be degraded, and its ability to turn the Flanks may be halted – the prospect of all of these may give the Soviets serious pause before undertaking, war and will complicate their ability to concentrate at the decisive center. Neither side, however, is under any illusion that our abilities at these points can overthrow Soviet power. Moreover, the ability to move maritime forces with some dispatch either in or out of an area reinforces their particularly deterrent qualities.

The maritime campaign being developed and exercised by Striking Fleet, Atlantic is an attempt to apply the forward strategy to the Norwegian Sea under given technological, geographical and political conditions. Variations and alternatives may be explored. As conditions change, basic elements of the campaign options could be modified. Its basic thrust is supportive both of the containment policy and of the forward strategy, though it is not identical with them. But it is a responsible and necessary development. If we fail to structure and exercise our forces in such a way as to improve our chances for victory in the Norwegian Sea and to pose a credible threat to targets that Soviets value, neither our political will nor our strategy can be taken seriously by the Soviets. Deterrence today, as historically, requires that we take warfighting seriously.

THE NORTHERN FLANK CAMPAIGN

Our deterrence posture is based on denial of Soviet objectives and, failing that, punishment. Because of the uncertain risk of escalation, this has thus far been an effective deterrent. Moreover, given the current force balance in Central Europe, General Rogers has characterized his options as 'escalate or capitulate'. In either case, however, war termination with Warsaw Pact forces on NATO territory would put in question the *raison d'être* of the Alliance and may well result in the Soviets achieving their fundamental aim of the dissolution of NATO. Furthermore, escalation to nuclear weapons may not prove to NATO's military advantage. The threat of intercontinental exchange as part of our deterrent posture may be persuasive. But in the event of war itself we may prefer a broader set of options, since it is unclear how such a strike would reverse the battlefield situation in Europe.

Compared to a strategy of either escalating to nuclear warfare or capitulation, a strategy that allows global, conventional, and extended warfare has merit both from a deterrent and warfighting perspective. Such an approach maximizes the utility of the economic and human potential of the West, and does not convert an initial loss of NATO territory into either the dissolution of the Alliance or Armageddon.

It would remain true that the nuclear dimension of even a prolonged conventional war between NATO and the Warsaw Pact would remain paramount. In the first place, the Soviets may well view conventional warfighting as a stage that precedes nuclear war, and would have fighting the war for the nuclear advantage a foremost objective (i.e., the strategic balance at the conclusion of fighting). Moreover, the existence of a large proportion of dual-capable systems (as well as nuclear systems that are indistinguishable from conventional systems) implies that even conventional exchanges will necessarily result in the reduction of nuclear forces, and could thus shift elements of the nuclear balance. Second, because Soviet general purpose forces have the protection of their strategic nuclear forces (as well as their borders) as a primary mission, any threat to these targets should reduce the Soviet forces available to contest NATO command of the sea and perhaps prevent the commitment of some forces to the central land campaign. Soviet concerns for the strategic balance and for the ability to control theater combat with assigned forces may not only reinforce our deterrent posture in peacetime, but may well provide a basis for a negotiated termination of war should it occur.

Central to such a strategic perspective are Alliance cohesion and willingness to take the necessary steps to assert (and maintain) command of the seas. Control of Northern Norway is vital to establishing command of the Norwegian Sea and the North Atlantic, as is control of the Baltic Straits. Particularly in the far North, applications of maritime and air power initially contributes to the command of the seas necessary for the defense of the Central Front and ultimately provides NATO with an option to escalate Soviet risks short of the use of nuclear weapons. To make credible such a posture, we must exercise in peacetime our combined forces to indicate the capability to deploy early and aggressively, and the will to do so. As has been pointed out many times, this capability and will does not mean a foolhardy rush of surface forces into the Norwegian Sea but a sea, land, and air campaign partially sequential in character. The viability of various mixes and sequences requires intense campaign planning, gaming, and exercises now.

To prevent Soviet control of the vital sea and air spaces translates into control not only of the Norwegian Sea and the Baltic Straits but of the Bosphorus and the Japanese Straits as well. Discussion of the latter is beyond the scope of this chapter and control of the Baltic and its Straits primarily rests with the Danish, the German, the Swedish and the Norwegian forces. This control is probably more threatened by Warsaw Pact advances through Schleswig-Holstein and Jutland than by the Soviet Baltic Fleet. The success of Soviet and Warsaw Pact forces in Jutland compared to the success of Soviet forces in Northern Norway may in the event determine where naval power projection forces are best directed. Given the difficulty and dangers of these choices, a set of campaign options clearly needs to be developed and exercised.

Should NATO forces hold the littorals on the Norwegian Sea, sea control could be established in the Northern Norwegian Sea without the presence of a carrier battleforce. In this circumstance, Soviet surface forces and submarines west of North Cape could be defeated by NATO SSNs and Maritime Patrol Aircraft (armed with Harpoon) assisted by land-based reconnaissance and naval attack aircraft, while those submarines south of the GIN Gap were worked over by the full range of NATO ASW forces. Soviet surface combatants are not likely to be in the Atlantic at the start of hostilities. An important point to keep in mind is that Soviet attack submarines in the North Atlantic will have a priority for targets. Anti-SSBN and anti-carrier missions are expected to be top priorities, followed by strategic cruise missile and sea lane interdiction missions. Keeping SSBN, CVBG and convoys geographically separated would prevent Soviet submarines from accomplishing more than one mission at a time, and would permit NATO forces to concentrate on the area where they were aggregated to accomplish their priority mission.

Presumed in the situation above is that defenses in Northern Norway hold, the air bases remain largely intact, and that there are sufficient sorties for land-based aircraft to conduct close air support, defensive (and perhaps offensive) counter-air, and battlefield-air interdiction, and also to conduct strikes at sea against Soviet amphibious and other naval forces. Should the available aircraft and facilities not be able to support all of these missions, the Atlantic Fleet Striking Force may be the best alternative available to carry on the battle. Though the time of year and weather will largely determine the pace of events this far north, should there be any shortfall in the USAF, USMC or Canadian aircraft assigned to the region, support from the Striking Force may be required immediately for the successful defense of Northern Norway.

Just as control of Northern Norway assures NATO control of the Norwegian Sea, control of the Norwegian Sea is necessary to sustain the fight in Northern Norway. Limited facilities will tax the logistics pipeline in a future battle as they did in the Second World War. Movement by sea is the only viable means of supplying the material needed. Therefore we cannot afford to think of the Norwegian Sea as the Soviet's backyard, too risky a place to operate. It seems perverse to think of a sea whose only littorals are NATO territory as under Soviet purview. The risk is in not committing enough forces to what is admittedly a relatively small theater of conflict compared to the central front, but which has such strategic significance.

Should the war begin under conditions where neither forward defenses nor Alliance cohesion are likely to hold, the strategy must call for something else to achieve termination acceptable to NATO. A polar view of the world reveals another aspect of the strategic importance of the north. From waters contiguous to the Soviet Union the newer classes of Soviet SSBNs can target their missiles under the protection of their own naval forces and ice. Reversing the direction, the flight path from strategic bomber bases in the US to Moscow passes right over the Kola Peninsula. In addition to their role as protectors of SSBNS, with the introduction of fourth generation aircraft, the surface forces of the Soviet Northern Fleet play an increasing role in extending the Northern air defense zone against strategic bomber attack. Destruction of both the SSBNs and their covering forces affect the Soviet calculation of the nuclear balance. Regarded principally as strategic reserve, the loss of Soviet warheads at sea directly affects targetting and the Soviets perception of their ability to prevail should the US launch a first strike. A reduction in air defenses also enters into the calculations through the increasing number of bombers and cruise missiles that could penetrate the Soviet Union to their targets.

To some extent, operations to gain control of the sea affect the nuclear balance by reducing the total forces available to the Soviets to commit to strategic defense. However, should the situation warrant, specifically assigning NATO SSNs to the destruction of Northern Fleet strategic forces operating in the Barents and under the ice would directly alter the nuclear balance and raise Soviet risks associated with not reaching a termination agreement.

The employment of any of the above options or others that may develop in some aspects dependent on three operational requirements: (i) early deployment of Striking Fleet, Atlantic; (ii) operations in the Norwegian leads and fjords to reduce and counter the threat to our forward-deployed forces; and (iii) employment of the combined might of Striking Fleet carriers, ASW forces, amphibious forces and marines, and land-based air.

As noted early, if the key battle for the control of the North develops early, in both deterrent and warfighting terms it is important that NATO respond to warning in a timely and orderly way by the early deployment of maritime forces. Such early deployment requires attention to the defense of the forces and hence recent attention to co-ordination of land- and sea-based air defense. Operating in Norwegian territorial waters prior to hostilities also excludes Soviet forces, thus reducing the prospect of pre-emption. The submarine threat may remain the most difficult. But deployment adjacent to Norway has the added advantage of allowing the Striking Fleet to concentrate its ASW forces in small areas, heightening the prospect of success. The recent exercise Ocean Safari 85 further suggested the importance and feasibility of operating with allies and exploiting geography to reduce the threat. With the attrition of the immediate threat, the striking power of the combined forces could indeed be formidable.

Critics of the Striking Fleet Atlantic's concept of operations may be missing the point. If containment remains the policy of the NATO allies and the forward strategy is the cohesive cement of the Alliance in both political and military terms, there are few acceptable alternatives but to develop and test these various options. No one can predict what combination of forces and options would be used at the moment of battle. The political and military context will be decisive. The improvement of one's ability to survive and operate aggressively in this area is, however, an important element of deterrence and provides the campaign discipline to respond flexibly in the event of war.

Note

1. See Robert S. Wood and John T. Hanley, Jr. 'The Maritime Role in the North Atlantic', *Naval War College Review*, November–December 1985: 5–18.

8 A German View
Commander F. U. Kupferschmidt

A number of significant events in the past decade have had an impact on NATO's maritime strategy and have therefore influenced German naval concepts. These events occurred both in and out of area, and showed the vulnerability of developed societies to attempts to outflank their traditional defence posture. The oil crisis, the Soviet invasion of Afghanistan, the Iran–Iraq war, and above all the impressive development of Soviet maritime power, with global options and capabilities that were demonstrated so explicitly in Summerex 85. In Germany, these events helped to switch the focus to some extent from the Central Front to the Northern Flank; its importance for European defence is now more widely recognized.

CHANGES IN GERMAN NAVAL CONCEPTS

In particular, the Soviet naval build-up over the last two decades led to a change in the assessment of the threat, and had therefore great influence on naval conceptual planning in the Federal Republic of Germany. In the late 1950s and during the 1960s, in the face of a Soviet fleet more or less restricted to coastal waters, we concentrated our contribution to the defence posture of the Alliance very much on the Baltic approaches.

But then the perspective widened: with the growing potential of the Northern Fleet and the impressive Soviet submarine fleet in mind, the tasks in the North Sea and Baltic were given the same weight, and later on, the defence of the Northern Flank as a whole became more significant.[1]

In June 1980 the Federal Security Council lifted the self-imposed national operational restrictions on our naval forces. Since then they have been operating more often beyond 61° North and the Dover–Calais line. The decision takes account of the inherent flexibility of naval assets and their envisaged employment as documented in the Defence Policy Guidelines and the White Paper of 1979.[2] This lifting of restrictions was generally welcomed, particularly in the light of the Soviet invasion into Afghanistan and the resulting commitment of US naval forces to regions outside the NATO treaty area; it thus represented a contribution to enhanced NATO flexibility.

Today, the defence of the Northern Flank region plays a prominent part in the strategy of the Alliance. It is not only to be seen as a commitment by the other NATO members towards Denmark, Norway and Iceland but also a very important element in the forward defence of Europe at its seaflank; it is, indeed, the decisive forward defence for the Atlantic.

Not only from the Soviet point of view is the strength of the Alliance ultimately based on the linkage between North America and Europe, the old continent is so dependent on the new for reinforcements. If we look at the threat and NATO's defence against it, we see a fundamental disparity between NATO and the Warsaw Pact. The territory of the Soviet Union is directly adjacent to that of her allies and lies only 650 km away from the Central European borderline between West and East. In contrast, North American reinforcements have to cross a 6000-km wide 'maritime gap' – the Atlantic Ocean – in order to reach European NATO territory.

The Federal Republic of Germany is particularly affected by this geostrategic asymmetry, for its territory is confronted with the bulk of the most combat-effective ground and air forces of the Warsaw Pact. From north to south the Federal Republic stretches over approximately 800 km, but it is on average only 225 km from east to west. So Germany lies like a narrow barrier across the main avenues of advance of the Warsaw Pact. Approximately one-third of our population and about 23 per cent of our industrial potential are crammed into a 100-km wide strip adjacent to the border. Even small losses of territory would seriously endanger what we need to preserve.

THE SOVIET THREAT

The threat posed by the potential of Soviet maritime, air and land forces in the North results primarily from the fact that, unlike that of NATO, it is available for offensive purposes against the geographically or structurally most vulnerable points of the Alliance.

The principle of Forward Defence cannot be implemented successfully unless the Alliance is able to deploy sufficient American reinforcements across the Atlantic to Europe. Similar conditions apply to the holding of maritime key positions on the flanks of NATO such as

Northern Norway, the Baltic Approaches, Gibraltar and the Turkish Straits.

It must therefore be of the highest priority for the Soviet Union to disrupt NATO's Sea Lines of Communication (SLOCs) across the Atlantic and into the Northern Flank area. The achievement of this objective would require securing control of the Baltic Approaches and Northern Norway, allowing the Warsaw Pact to combine the fighting potential of the Baltic and Northern Fleets. This would much improve their chances of attacking Allied reinforcement and resupply shipping successfully. A second objective linked to the improvement of the geostrategic situation of the Northern Fleet is the protection of the Soviet ballistic missile submarines and of the Kola Peninsula itself. In the view of the Soviet Union this, of course, must give very high significance to the Northern Region.

For some years NATO has been aware of the threat posed by the growing Soviet maritime potential. The Alliance's most significant reaction to this grave situation is the 'Concept of Maritime Operations' paper agreed by the three major NATO Commanders. The three principles set out in this document are for:

1. Containment of the Warsaw Pact Fleets
2. Defence in depth
3. Keeping the initiative.

The European members are happy with this statement of maritime policy. It should, however, be kept in mind, that there is a distinct functional interdependence between the operational principles just mentioned and the forces available for their implementation.

The timely deployment of American Carrier Battle Groups into the Norwegian Sea would be one of the key elements in the struggle to gain sea control in the Northern Flank area, and is a prerequisite for the unconstrained reinforcement and resupply sea traffic to Europe.

Whether the decision for deployment of the Carrier Battle Groups and for reinforcements would be taken early enough is, however, open to speculation. It hinges very much on the overall political situation prevailing at that time. Some recent exercises produced quite encouraging results in this respect, but in real life politicians may be rather reluctant to endorse these plans at a sufficiently early stage in the crisis or confrontation. So initially Europe would possibly have to contain the Soviets with its own forces.

The Federal Republic of Germany has declared her willingness to join forces with her allies up North and has dedicated a considerable number of units – namely, destroyers, frigates, maritime patrol aircraft and mine countermeasures vessels – to the respective operational plans. The bigger patrol submarines planned to enter service in the 1990s are a contribution especially tailored for the requirements of the Northern Flank.

To demonstrate to the Soviets NATO's interest in the freedom of the Northern waters, a more prominent Allied naval presence should be seen in this area. I am thinking of more European as well as American ships, although unfortunately an increased US naval activity is too often solely perceived in the context of the global bilateral competition between the two Superpowers.

In the Baltic, a clearly visible naval presence of countries not neighbouring these waters is necessary from time to time, to demonstrate against the notorious and continuous Soviet endeavour to make a closed sea out of it.

Unfortunately, not all member nations in NATO seem as yet prepared to give practical approval to the fact that the Northern Flank is a strategic entity; compartmentation tends to hamper efforts to bring to bear the strength of naval assets wherever the situation demands. It therefore seems logical that campaign options be developed for the Carrier Battle Groups and US amphibious forces for Northern Norway as well as for Jutland. Enhancing NATO's defence posture in the Northern Flank also requires joint planning, especially as the command boundaries of the three Major North Commanders (MNCs) are adjacent to each other. The conclusion of the 'TRI-MNC Agreement on Maritime Operations in the North Sea and Adjacent Waters' marked a milestone within the field of operational planning because it eased cross-boundary operations. The TRI-MNC Plan 'Fence-Breaker' represents another promising step in the right direction. This should now be followed by a joint effort by CINCEASTLANT and CINCNORTH – on behalf of their major NATO commanders – to harmonize their respective General Defence Plans (GDPs). A joint plan for wartime operations (i.e., a Joint Maritime GDP) would seem to follow on logically from the idea of a Concept of Maritime Operations.

THE GERMAN CONTRIBUTION

The Federal Republic of Germany borders the region of the Northern

Flank and parts of her territory and her sea lines of communication extend into this area. Over and above her commitments within the Alliance, the Federal Republic of Germany has a vital national interest in this region, as already stated in the White Paper of 1979:

> The Federal Republic of Germany has a vital interest in safeguarding the security of NATO's geostrategical key positions at its Northern Flank.[3]

The German contribution to the defence of the Northern Flank is mainly (but not exclusively) maritime. The German Army and Air Force contribute considerably to the defence of Schleswig-Holstein and the Baltic Approaches. Assigned to COMBALTAP forces, they have to take up defence positions as far to the east as possible, attacking amphibious and air landings executed in conjunction with attacks on advancing Warsaw Pact land forces. German army forces assigned to COMBALTAP comprise a heavy armoured division and a home defence brigade. The Air Force contributes to the defence of the Northern Flank with two squadrons each of reconnaissance and fighter bomber aircraft. The defense of the COMBALTAP area is seen as a protective barrier in front of the air defence regions of Southern Norway, and to a degree also of the United Kingdom against any threat emanating from the east.

As maritime forward defence cannot be tied to boundaries of specific areas, it calls for naval and naval air forces to be employed as the situation demands and wherever the enemy launches or develops his attacks. The numerical superiority of the enemy afloat in the Northern Flank area requires that full use is made of the depth of the area to engage him early and repeatedly, so as to wear him out by attrition; it also requires that geographical conditions be exploited to block him off wherever possible.

The Federal Republic's share within the maritime defence posture[4] of the six north-west European navies amounts to roughly one-third. In the Baltic, it carries the main burden of the maritime defence, providing approximately three-quarters of the naval forces and all the naval air power in this area. But we must always ensure that the German navy does not become so dominant in the defence of the Baltic that an adversary might try, by challenging just us, to single out one country. That is why we are so interested in Denmark maintaining the level and composition of her naval forces.

To the east of Bornholm, the enemy's offensive capabilities must be weakened, and it must be made difficult for him to use the sea as an area for initial deployment and as a supply route. For this task, only those naval resources can be employed that are capable of either operating undetected or which can penetrate strong enemy defences. Accordingly our defence in depth is based on 24 small, silent patrol submarines, equipped with modern wire-guided torpedoes and a considerable minelaying capacity, and 112 Tornado Fighter Bomber of the Naval Air Arm equipped with up to four Kormoran air-to-surface-missiles each.

In the Baltic Approaches area, the use of lines of communication from and to the Atlantic must be secured for friendly operations, and denied to the enemy. Friendly forces, exposed to a permanent air threat, must repel enemy amphibious forces and raiding parties and carry out mine countermeasures. Small, agile combat units capable of taking advantage of the numerous islands, bays and straits to avoid detection and to use their weapons for surprise attacks are best suited for this purpose, given the conditions prevailing in this area.

Naval fighter bombers, fast patrol boats, light minelayers or minesweepers and helicopters are vested with these capabilities. We are especially confident of the merits and performance of our 40 combat craft with 160 MM 38 Exocet between them. Some of the boats are equally fitted with wire-guided torpedoes and (later on) will receive an anti-ship missile defence system. Sea King helicopters with Sea Skua ASMs will soon reinforce German naval warfare capacity. Some 40 minesweepers ensure that sea-lines and harbour approaches are kept navigable while 32 medium and small landing craft contribute their share to operational mobility of Allied land forces in this area.

In the North Sea and Norwegian Sea, enemy forces must not be allowed to deploy fully and break through to the Atlantic and Southern North Sea, where they would severely threaten friendly coasts, troop transports and supply shipments. This task would be best discharged by repelling enemy submarines, aircraft and surface forces as far north and close to their bases as possible. The far-flung and the close covering operations required for this purpose both call for sufficient sea endurance, long ranges, mobility and all-weather capability. Destroyers and general purpose frigates, in fact our whole escort fleet including auxiliaries and helicopters, new submarines, ASW and long-range maritime patrol aircraft and naval fighter bombers, are dedicated to the common defence of this sea area. Destroyers and frigates could be employed in multi-purpose task groups in escort or area operations supported by Tornados in reconnaissance and attack missions, while submarines and our maritime patrol aircraft could take part in barrier operations.

The German Fleet is particularly mobile, as it can rely on an important logistic support afloat comprising more than 25 auxiliaries. It thus is well prepared for prolonged deployments further away from its home bases. In a few years time all but one of our 16 destroyers and frigates will deploy either Harpoon or Exocet SSMs; 11 of them will be equipped with either Sea Sparrow or Standard Missile SAMs. Along with the Tornado naval fighter bombers this force is a very substantial contribution indeed to the defence of the Northern Flank.

In the North Sea, mines are a further threat we have to deal with. Mining of the shallow waters can be carried out by enemy aircraft and submarines. Our modern MCM forces (12 minehunters and 6 Troika systems[5]) are tasked to keep harbour approaches and shipping routes open and to support US reinforcement transports in order to ensure their safe arrival ashore.

The significance of the problems pointed out here would seem somewhat reduced at the present time since there appears to be no acute danger of an armed conflict; however patterns and trends must not be neglected. All the more attention should be paid to the ever-growing importance of the Soviet Navy, the primary objective of which is the disruption of the Allied SLOCs. If the Soviets were to succeed, the credibility of deterrence and the capability for conventional defence in Europe would suffer a severe blow. To a large extent NATO depends on its Northern Flank for the deflection of that possible blow; if all actual programmes for *materiel* improvements are achieved, if an agreement on joint defence planning is reached, and if the defence burden were spread more evenly, then I think – modern and capable as our Allied forces are – we would stand a fair chance of succeeding.

Notes

1. Compare Federal Minister of Defence, *White Paper 1979*, pp. 176–7 and *White Paper 1985*, pp. 213–18.
2. *White Paper 1979*, para. 224, p. 176.
3. *White Paper 1979*, para 225, p. 176; *White Paper 1985*, pp. 213–17.
4. *White Paper 1985*, pp. 218–22.
5. Each TROIKA system consists of one control vessel and three remotely-controlled unmanned sweeping units.

9 The Maritime Strategy: A Norwegian View
Captain Thor Nikolaisen (RNON)

It is quite clear that certain aspects of Norwegian security policy will change with the new Labour Government in Norway – perhaps not in substance, but certainly in terms of rhetoric and the way people are addressing certain problems. Such a change of government may happen in Britain too, in 1987 or 1988, and this will have an impact on security policy, though again not as large an impact as rhetoric may suggest. In the United States there have been changes in security policy as administrations have changed. It is therefore important to distinguish between what is rhetoric and what substance, between what changes and what does not.

Dr Wood in Chapter 7, has given a very good overview of the responses which the West ought to have been pursuing in the maritime arena in the past, and will need to pursue in the years ahead. Most aspects of the challenges we are facing in the endeavour to contain and dissuade the Soviet Union from taking actions detrimental to our interests have been set out in that chapter, in a logical and comprehensive manner. There is no disagreement with his emphasis on containment and the need for a forward military posture. Indeed, the fact that NATO was created and still exists as a viable organization is a proof of the perceived need for such a strategic philosophy. The attachment of similar countries like Norway and Turkey makes a policy of forward defence absolutely essential. It is part and parcel of what NATO is about, and is evidence that NATO is working, despite what scaremongers may have said.

Moreover, there should be no disagreement on his views about the linkage which exists between the Flanks and the Centre, and the importance of maritime forces in this connection. The linkage between the North and the Centre, and its historical continuity, was recently made clear in a report by the *Frankfurter Allgemeine Zeitung*:

> As early as 1905, at the time of the dissolution of the union between Norway and Sweden, the British Admiralty believed that: 'Should a Russian invasion of the North Norwegian province of Finnmark

enable Moscow to dominate the whole Scandinavian Peninsula – which must be assessed as a possibility in the future – then the very foundations of the balance of power in Europe would be shaken.' These very words were echoed some three generations later – in April 1981 – by Admiral Train of the United States, at that time NATO's Commander-in-Chief, Atlantic. He stated, in an interview given to the *Frankfurter Allgemeine Zeitung* that: 'Today, the Northern Flank is not secure. Should we lose the Northern Flank, we would not only lose one of the NATO members, Norway, but also the ability to bring reinforcements to Europe. Should this happen, then we would also have lost Germany.'

To have consensus in principle over such matters is all very well, but the problems arise when the details are sketched into the overall picture, for that is when concrete measures have to be undertaken, and when hard choices have to be made. Questions of priority and alternatives arise, and will have to be answered. In fact, the question of priorities is the crux of the matter.

Another set of questions which needs to be addressed is the real viability of a forward maritime strategy – especially in an early phase of a conflict at sea, when the Soviet Union has at its disposal intact naval and air forces. To what extent is it feasible to push forward with carrier strike groups and so forth before attrition has begun? From a technical point of view this is a real problem, but it has political connotations, too. One of the reasons why people back home have misgivings, especially about the rhetoric, is that they are not so sure that the Americans can make it stick. If they cannot make it stick, then maybe Norwegians will be left in the lurch. Moreover, up to 1979 the US Navy did not appear interested at all in this idea of a forward strategy. In fact, Norway had a role in its introduction because people like Dr Holst started to point out that we were creating a kind of *mare sovieticum* off the North, effectively by default, so something had to be done.

A particularly difficult part of this task, and I write as an ASW man myself, will be to meet the challenge posed by Soviet submarines. It will be a long drawn out conflict, maybe even lasting for months. Perhaps it will be just as it was in the Second World War when the British found that despite their early hopes of ASDIC they were facing a long and bitter struggle against German U-boats. If you have few carriers you will not want to commit them until the submarine threat has been brought under control; thinking of these things is being prudent, not faint-hearted. The Norwegians have after all supported the presence of US carriers in the North and indeed have had the *USS America* participating in military exercises in the Westfjorden area. But we still have niggling doubts about it all for operational reasons.

It is also important to discuss the crucial importance of the role which Britain plays in any type of campaign in the Norwegian Sea and on the Northern Flank. I am thinking of the contribution made by the Royal Marines and the role played by the Royal Navy and Royal Air Force. The British force of SSNs is a very effective one, even when compared to the size of the US Navy's submarine fleet (not least because half of it will be, with the end of the age of swing, serving in the Pacific anyway).

The British infrastructure will be important, too, particularly in the shape of its airfields, just as they were in the US operations against Libya. In this part of the world, the Americans cannot move without Britain. The bases and facilities in the United Kingdom are of crucial importance both for the Americans and to help Norway. Moreover, the British and the Europeans may not be able to manage the 'mostest', but they can at least manage the 'firstest'. We need to put some emphasis on the very fact that they are already here. In short, there is the strong possibility that in times of tension and in an unclear situation, the European (and in particular British) maritime forces, being as it were on the spot, would have to bear the brunt since major parts of US maritime forces may not be available, at least in an initial phase.

There is another aspect to the time factor which I think it is worthwhile elaborating on, namely who is going to prevail at sea in the longer term. Dr Wood has gone into this in Chapter 7 in terms of the nuclear balance – and the risks the Soviets run in a war at sea through the gradual attrition of their ballistic missile fleet. This must be a sobering thought for the Soviets, which is why personally I am in favour of it. But there is also a conventional aspect to this. If the West prevails at sea it is hard to see how the Soviets can hold on to (or consolidate) whatever footholds they have gained on the Northern Flank. If you look back to the Second World War some 8000 or 9000 German troops seized six ports, and the allies failed to get them out. But what is often forgotten is that immediately afterwards the Germans brought in another 110 000 troops, because the British were not masters of the Approaches to Norway. They ended up having 400 000 men in Norway during the war, because they never knew what the British would be up to next with a Fleet that was still intact. We should consider long-term aspects like this, because the question of husbanding of resources for a later phase of a war runs counter to risking the maritime assets in an initial phase. That logic may instill prudence, and could provide an additional leverage for NATO's deterrence.

10 A British View
Geoffrey Till

INTRODUCTION: THE CENTRE AND THE NORTH

The Northern region of the continent of Europe has for many centuries been of great political, military, economic and cultural interest to the United Kingdom.[1] Over the past several centuries, indeed, the orientation of Britain's maritime interest has been steadily shifting to the North, as the focus of hostility moved from the Spanish to the French and Dutch, and then the Germans at the beginning of this century. With the emergence of the Soviet Northern Fleet as Britain's principal maritime preoccupation, this process has simply gone one stage further.

But British attitudes to the North have nevertheless been uneven because the Northern threat was rarely the only one Britain faced even in Europe. The potential dilemma was in fact highlighted by the British geopolitician Halford Mackinder before and after the First World War. He warned that Britain 'must . . . reckon with the possibility that a large part of the Great Continent might someday be united under a single sway and that an invincible sea-power might be based upon it'.[2] First Germany essayed this role, then Russia. Its consequence was that it posed Britain two simultaneous threats, the first a land–air one from the East, the second a sea–air one from the North.

Not surprisingly, British strategists have tended to produce two traditions of defence policy to deal with the situation. The first is to emphasize the importance of the Central (or, in the terminology of the Generals of the First World War, the Western) Front, *vis-à-vis* peripheral less important areas to north and south. In the Second World War, such people argue, the *relative* unimportance of Norway was demonstrated by the fact that the Norwegian campaign only finally collapsed (when at Narvik it was at least beginning to go quite well) when France fell. Equally, Norway was bypassed and liberated in consequence of the fall of Nazi Germany, and not as a contribution to it.

In the same way, Britain's attitude towards the allocation of resources to the North is likely to be fundamentally determined by her conception of how well things are going in the Centre. When in the mid- to late 1970s it became fashionable to argue that within a couple of days of the war starting, the Soviet 3rd Shock Army would be rolling over the rubble of Bielefeld and Dortmund, it seemed hardly to matter what the 45th Motor Rifle Division was doing in Lapland. To analysts of that persuasion, the prospect of *independent* Soviet action in the North also seems arcane. As Peter Vigor has remarked:

> I have never yet read a Soviet book on strategy or operations art that has failed to stress the importance of putting a massive, the maximum possible, blow along the principal axis of advance, and the principal axis of advance from the Soviet Union's point of view . . . is due west, straight across West Germany.[3]

Moreover because the East–West balance on the Central Front seems so precarious, NATO is urged to guard itself from distraction. During the Norwegian campaign of 1940, Churchill wrote: 'The main remaining value of our forces in Norway is to entice and retain largely superior forces in that area, *away from the main decision*.'[4] Perhaps the Soviet High Command has similar ideas of luring NATO forces away from where, in the last analysis, they really matter?

Of course, none of this means that the North does *not* matter, merely that the Central Front must have priority when it comes to the allocation of reinforcements and resupplies. Moreover, effort on the Northern Flank is especially justifiable if it materially contributes to success in the Centre. The more speculative the linkages, the less certain the support for such operations and the greater the tendency to concentrate on the demands of the Centre. Given that defence resources are finite, this is bound to work to the disadvantage of the North.

The alternative tradition concedes the importance of the Central Front, but emphasizes the extent to which events there are dependent on the outcome of events in the North. The point was made recently by General Sir Steuart Pringle, then Commandant-General of the Royal Marines:

> Thus we in the Royal Marines regard Norway as being the forward edge of a potential battle of the Atlantic, rather than merely a peripheral area on the left flank of a land war on the centre front, a view which I believe is more clearly seen in Norfolk, Virginia than it is perhaps sometimes in Whitehall, London. However, I think it is fair to say that there does seem to be a growing conviction in UK defence circles, that the defence of NEC would be fundamental to

the success of the battle of the Atlantic and therefore, by extension, to any war in central Europe.[5]

Not unnaturally, this is a view which finds some favour in Scandinavia.

The natural preoccupation of this school of analysis is with the burgeoning power of the Soviet Union in the North, and in particular of the Soviet Northern Fleet based at Severomorsk. People of this persuasion tend to derive many of their arguments from geography; they maintain that Britain's own geography means that its concerns must be maritime. As an island critically dependent on sea-borne supplies and reinforcement, threats to its capacity to use the sea strike particularly deeply. Placed where they are, the British Isles are protected from direct assault by the intervening land masses of Western Europe and Scandinavia. The collapse of either would make Britain the new front line, a fate it has been the preoccupation of generations of British military men and diplomatists to prevent.

Like many others, this presentation doubtless makes the two traditions seem too competitive. In fact, both are right, and it is essential for British security that threats from North *and* Centre be countered. Since the requirements and implication of the two imperatives intertwine at every point, British naval attitudes towards the Far North reflect a good deal more than mere responses to the fact (and consequences) of a burgeoning Soviet Northern Fleet.

BRITISH NAVAL ACTIVITY IN PEACETIME

Of course, 'containing' the consequences of Soviet naval power is something that begins in peacetime. The fundamental business of defence after all is deterrence and war prevention. Being but a small island, the UK depend for its ultimate security against a much larger and more powerful adversary upon its Alliance with other countries. The UK's ultimate security thus rests on its ability to keep its Alliances in good order; anything that disrupts those Alliances therefore fundamentally threatens British security. Because of this it is important for Britain that her links with the United States and with Scandinavia be maintained, and since the gaps between them are filled with stretches of water, Alliance management in this area is a maritime preoccupation. The point was made in the Defence White Paper of 1975:

If the balance of maritime power were to shift so far in favour of the

Warsaw Pact that it had an evident ability . . . to isolate Europe by sea, the effect on Allied confidence and cohesion would be profound.[6]

Because unchallenged Soviet maritime predominance in the North would tend gradually to erode those linkages, it is important to 'answer' it with corresponding flag-showing manoeuvres.

The fact that improving the local correlation of forces by fragmenting the political–military cohesion of its adversaries is given such stress in Soviet strategic thinking reinforces the need for NATO members constantly to offer each other this kind of maritime reassurance. There is also much to be said for this low-level deterrence to be a task for interested Europeans rather than benign outsiders, however powerful they may be. Many of Britain's normal peacetime activities in the North are therefore held to be justified by the general contribution they make to deterrence and war prevention. If successful, they should prevent a conflict from breaking out in the first place. British air and sea patrols in northern waters signal interest in the area, and Britain's determination that the waters to the North do not become Russian by default. They also serve a multitude of surveillance and intelligence-gathering purposes.

CONTAINMENT IN WAR

Northern waters are a kind of 'two-way street', making it possible for the Soviet Union's Navy and merchant ships to reach the oceans of the world, but at the same time providing a means which that country's adversaries might use to come and attack her territory or to seek to interfere with her use of the seas around her shores. Exactly the same thing applies to the Western powers, of course. Northern waters are strategically important therefore not so much for themselves as for what their control makes possible.

The British perspective on this is fairly simple. Both as a maritime power heavily dependent on merchant shipping and as a rearward base for operations on the continent of Europe, Britain needs secure Sea Lines of Communication (SLOCs) across the Atlantic and over to the mainland of Europe. She needs protection against all forms of sea-based attack (whether these be offensive mining campaigns, amphibious raids, Spetsnaz operations, cruise and ballistic missile attack, etc.). Her own SSBNs need, in Soviet terminology, sufficient 'combat stability' for them to perform their tasks – and so, for that matter, do her fishing vessels, her offshore oil and gas installations and so on.

Individually and/or in concert with her allies, Britain would seek to protect her capacity to use the sea in all these varied ways by contesting the control of Northern waters with the Soviet Union. The greater the extent of sea control won (or lost) the more (or less) the British and their allies can use the sea for these purposes and deny this same facility to the Soviet Union.

For this reason British and other European navies would engage in a wide and varied complex of operations designed to 'contain' the Soviet Fleet. Aircraft and submarines could well be deployed forward to engage targets with bombs, missiles, torpedoes and mines; behind them would be barrier operations across the choke points (most notably the Bear Island–North Cape line and the GIUK Gap). Further back still, Soviet units would encounter the point defences around British and other allied assets at sea including reinforcement shipping coming across the Atlantic, and a final last defence of British sea and air space. The whole point of NATO's naval strategy (and of the Royal Navy's place in it), in short, is to offer a defence in depth. There can be little doubt that serious failure in this policy of containment would gravely disrupt almost anything NATO would seek to do in a serious and sustained conflict.

HOLDING THE FORT

In a conflict the British, together with most of the other countries of north-western Europe, accept that there may well be a period in which they will need to 'hold the fort' until the American Strike Fleet arrives. As the 1985 British Defence White Paper puts it:

> It must be assumed that only limited US Navy forces would be available in the Eastern Atlantic at the outbreak of hostilities. European Navies, and in particular the Royal Navy, must therefore be ready to play a leading role in initial operations.[7]

Two things suggest that Europeans need not be overly pessimistic about their prospects of success in this initial period of containment of Soviet naval power. First of all, it is reasonable to expect that the Soviet Navy would, at least to begin with, be quite cautious in its attempt to break out into the open oceans, partly because it would have enough to do in home waters anyway and partly in due deference to its geographic and climatic disadvantages. Moreover, the Soviet Northern Fleet would be rather in the position of the British Grand Fleet in the first two years of the First World War. It would be reluctant to press home an attack against weaker forces, lest by doing so it frittered away its superiority before the main opponent, the US Navy (filling in this respect the role of Scheer's battle fleet in that earlier conflict) arrived on the scene. So the forces of the north-west Europeans should at least be able to prevent the Soviet Union from achieving a *fait accompli*, provided their surveillance capacities are good enough to prevent their being taken totally by surprise.

Second, this conclusion is reinforced by a look at the resources that the British and their allies have for this kind of holding operation. The British for instance, have two squadrons of Buccaneers at RAF Lossiemouth currently armed with Martel and laser-guided bombs, but shortly to be fitted with the very effective Sea Eagle. It is also intended to fit Harpoon missiles to the RAF's Nimrod force. Operating from northern Scotland, or from Norwegian airfields, these aircraft would give a Soviet force commander some considerable food for thought should he think of straying into their area. The Royal Navy also operates a substantial force of submarines that are particularly useful in Northern waters because, in the words of a recent Vice-Chief of the Naval Staff:

> They are our best anti-submarine platform; their covert nature allows them to operate in circumstances where the enemy has achieved air and surface superiority; the threat which they pose is an undefined one which, lacking as he does any certain knowledge, an enemy must assume to be continuously present wherever he is and whatever he is doing. These characteristics are, of course, particularly embodied in the nuclear submarine with its unlimited endurance and mobility free of logistic support.[8]

Submarines would also figure extensively in Britain's contribution to air and barrier operations against Soviet submarines coming south through the gaps. The American Sound Surveillance System (SOSUS), a system of passive hydrophone arrays laid on the seabed, monitors the area, and its detection capacity would be supplemented by Britain's Nimrod maritime patrol aircraft which deploy and control active and passive sonar buoys and which will be able to attack detected submarines with the new Stingray anti-submarine torpedo.

Below them would doubtless be the surface ships of the Royal Navy deploying ASW helicopters and both hull-mounted and towed sonar arrays. Currently the UK provide 70 per cent of the standing forces dedicated to the prosecution of submarines in the eastern and northern Atlantic. The Royal Navy's reputation for ASW efficiency is second to none, and the deployment of towed array sonar systems in its new batch Type 22 and Type 23 frigates, its battle-proved Invincible class and the new highly sophisticated EH 101 helicopter are expected to help maintain that reputation in the future. The advent of passive sonars in surface ships is a particular advantage since it extends detection ranges and denies warning to the submarine which therefore has less chance of taking countermeasures. It has to be said however that Soviet submarine technology and capacity are advancing too; the task of containing them is not likely to become any easier.

Since the Soviet Union could most certainly enhance its capacity to attack other NATO areas to the South or West by a successful *démarche* against Norway, the defence of the Northern part of that country is a part of the defence of Britain. Helping to deter or resist such an attack would obviously therefore be an important part of any operations designed to 'hold the fort' until the Americans arrived. This would clearly involve the British and other European navies in the considerable task of protecting and transporting sea-borne reinforcements to Norway and subsequently supporting them in their operations ashore.

THE FORWARD DEFENCE OF THE UK BASE

The last ring in this defensive system would be the point defence of the air and sea space around the British Isles themselves. The frequency with which British air space is probed by Soviet aircraft in itself provides every justification for the current build-up in British air defence with the Tornado F2. Just as important, the Soviet mining threat to the shipping routes around the British Isles and in the approaches to the ports expected to receive reinforcements and resupply from across the Atlantic argues the need for enhanced mine clearance. As has recently been remarked:

> Mine counter-measures capability . . . is a must in an island like ours. MCM effectiveness, in terms of keeping ports and harbours open, and of ensuring the uninterrupted deployment of the British as well as elements of the US ballistic missile submarine forces, is a major plank of our deterrent posture.[9]

The general decline in European MCM capacity over the past decade or so adds point to this remark.

Modern technology provides the other task which the Royal Navy might seek to perform in Northern waters, which in some way is a continuance of its historic 'wooden walls of England' role, namely the defence of the realm against sea-based nuclear attack. The deterrent aspiration of its own Polaris/Trident submarine force is obvious, but there may be a more directly defensive role here too. Northern waters, and very possibly Northern coastlines, would certainly be the deployment areas of Soviet SSBNs and very likely of Soviet submarines armed with the new and forthcoming SS-NX-21 and SS-NX-24 submarine-launched land attack cruise missiles. Since a proportion of these would certainly be targeted against the British Isles, there is at least a *prima facie* case that the Royal Navy should seek to destroy them.

Two arguments are deployed against such notion; first that such action against the adversary's strategic reserve would be provocative and destabilizing; second that Soviet force levels are so huge that attrition is unlikely to reduce the Soviet nuclear threat to the UK to a level the British would find 'acceptable' anyway, so the whole effort would be pointless. There is plainly something in both these arguments. However, there is also much to be said *for* such a campaign as well. Being able to threaten something the Soviet Union values would surely increase the deterrent, war-prevention effectiveness of the Royal Navy; more particularly such a threat could force the Soviet Navy to deploy assets to protect its SSBNs and SSGNs which might otherwise be available to damage British interests elsewhere. If the British did *deliberately* decide to undertake such a campaign (rather than prosecute such submarines inadvertently, for example in the course of barrier operations intended to protect Atlantic shipping) the sophisticated attack submarines and advanced means of ASW they need for other purposes would presumably be available, at least to an extent, for this task as well.

OPERATIONS WITH THE STRIKE FLEET

Currently, Britain deploys 2–3 ASW carriers, 53 front-line destroyers and frigates, four squadrons of Nimrods, and about 29 submarines all told. The precise allocation of these deepwater assets between the competing demands of forward deployment, barrier operations and area/point defence around the UK or around UK shipping would be a matter of fine judgement, depending absolutely on the details of the scenario envisaged. The ability of British planners to make useful predictions is lessened by fundamental uncertainty about when the US Navy's contribution would arrive, and what it would be found to comprise. Here the Americans' natural preference for flexibility acts against the planning interests of their European allies. The same applies, moreover, to the quite fundamental question of what the US Navy would do once it did arrive, because this will play a major role in determining European naval roles as well. If American assets were simply made available across the whole spectrum of containment operations one could expect much enhanced NATO performance at every level. But there is of course the real possibility that the US Navy would instead seek at some stage to concentrate its efforts on launching carrier strikes against the main sources of Soviet Naval power in the Kola Peninsula.

There is, of course, some scepticism about whether it is politically wise to prepare for this in peacetime, or strategically wise to try it in war. Because British and other Allied navies would certainly be involved in the campaign to support the local air and submarine threat (either as a preliminary or an alternative to such carrier operations) and because some of them may well operate in direct support of the US Navy (for example by providing ASW assets), this debate about the role of US Navy's carrier force is effectively one about theirs too. But as this chapter has tried to show, it will also be fundamentally affected by the debate about the likely nature and consequences of the campaign on the Central Front as well.

Notes

1. An early version of this paper appeared in *Fladestrategier og nordisk sikkerhedspolitik* (Copenhagen: SNU, 1986).
2. H. J. Mackinder, *Democratic Ideals and Reality* (London: Constable, 1919) p. 42.
3. In Lars B. Wallin (ed.), *The North Flank in a Central European War* (Stockholm: Swedish National Defence Research Institute, 1980).
4. Churchill to First Sea Lord, 20 May 1940, Prem. 328/10, Public Record Office.
5. In his 'Power Projection and the Role of the Royal Marines', in G. Till (ed.), *The Future of British Sea Power* (London: Macmillan, 1984) p. 152.

6. 1975, Statement of Defence Estimates, Cmd. 5976, pp. 9–10.
7. 1985, Statement of Defence Estimates, Cmd. 9430, p. 53.
8. Vice-Admiral Sir Peter Stanford, 'The Current Position of the Royal Navy' in Till (ed.), *The Future of British Sea Power*, p. 36.
9. Till (ed.), *The Future of British Sea Power* p. 37.

Conference Discussion

The Forward Strategy emerged conveniently as a special supplement to the Proceedings of the US Naval Institute in January 1986, but has not appeared over the signature of the Joint Chiefs of Staff. So one question that needs to be asked is: to what extent is it actually new and generally agreed? It fits in broadly with NATO's Concept of Maritime Operations, which has for some time emphasized the need for keeping the initiative, containment of hostile forces and forward movement as the principles behind what NATO should do at sea, especially in the waters north of the GIUK Gap.

There has, however, been a dramatic shift in the American strategic environment in the past year or two. About eighteen months ago, Admiral Stansfield Turner said in a radio broadcast that he did not know of a single US Navy Admiral who agreed with Forward Operations; now it is hard to find one that does not. This is because the idea itself has changed with the joint-service and coalition aspects of it now being given much more prominence.

Of course, a NATO strategy and a United States' national strategy are not the same because the United States has permanent, global interests. Because of such interests the Maritime Strategy will very likely become a consistent part of the national strategy of the United States, unless there is a major political or economic upset before 1990. The extent to which this shift is accepted is indicated by the way that such past critics as Robert Komer and James Schlesinger have come round to it. One of the reasons for this is that they now see that, for all that it is a national strategy, the emphasis now is on the fullest co-operation with America's allies.

The same is true at the interservice level where the US Navy is now much less unilateral than it used to be, and much more interested in working with the other services. This is reflected in policy formulations and joint service documents. National Security Document 32, for example has been much influenced by this kind of thinking. One of the most dramatic changes brought about by this has been the conversion of General Rogers who started out by being downright hostile, and is now supportive.

Many professionals also now accept that there are strong operational reasons for going North; what is at stake up there is a good deal more than the defence of Norway. It may well turn out that

NATO does not have the naval resources to maintain a flow of shipping across the Atlantic by simply staying south of the GIUK Gap and fighting a defensive campaign there. Furthermore, the option of staying out, and coming back later, may not in fact be open to the Alliance.

Being seen as being able to conduct Forward Operations would, in any case, make an important contribution to a peacetime strategy of deterrence. Its value lies in the fact that it can turn the tables on the Soviet Union by being able to put at risk something they value, namely their naval forces, the Kola Peninsula or indeed, their SSBNs. In some ways, though, there is a certain amount of discrepancy between the particular idea of going after SSBNs and the provisional guidelines behind NATO doctrine. Nevertheless, the US Navy has been targeting SSBNs long before this strategy was enunciated, so the maritime strategy is less of a change in this respect than is often thought. The perceived need to conduct anti-SSBN operations comes from America's conception of what is in its own national strategic interest, as well as the collective interest of the NATO Alliance.

Some analysts argue that the capacity to trail and target SSBNs and to be able to put on attack solutions is certainly needed; whether this capacity is exercised in a war would be a political more than a maritime decision. But the Soviet Union probably does not make much distinction between this kind of surveillance and targeting. As part of their conventional offensive into Western Europe, the Soviet Army, after all, intends in the conventional phase of the war to take out NATO's nuclear targets. Ogarkov has argued vigorously that a successful campaign of this sort will prevent the war going to an intercontinental nuclear phase. Given Soviet thinking on the matter, what is sauce for the goose is sauce for the gander. However much one might like to, in practice it is impossible to separate the conventional quite cleanly from the nuclear.

Another argument is that success in the anti-SSBN campaign would force the Soviet Union to use SSBNs it might otherwise simply lose. But this would simply be irrational. The real point about this is that a proper strategy of deterrence has also to think about war termination. How is this war to be ended? Certainly not by marching to Moscow, or trying to overthrow the Soviet Empire in Eastern Europe. Perhaps attacking their SSBNs would show them that the costs of carrying on would be worse than the costs of coming to an accommodation.

Yet another point of criticism is that anti-SSBN operations are just another sign of the kind of 'Rambo rhetoric' associated with the whole of the maritime strategy. Sometimes this rhetoric is said to be much more to do with the battle of the Potomac, than it is with the battle for the Barents. That is to say it is seen as a product of the struggle for a 600-ship navy rather than with operational realities. But the rhetoric is presented in ways that create political problems in Europe, and raise doubts in the minds of professionals about how feasible it all is.

On the other hand, there is more to it than merely a shift in presentation, conducted essentially for domestic political reasons. It may well reflect a profound strategic shift in American thinking; it may simply highlight the different cultural approaches to strategic thinking in the United States and in Europe. Although in view of this there may be a case for saying nothing at all, if it is going to cause controversy, there remains the need to talk professionally to one's own people in the US Navy and with one's allies.

Another problem on the matter of presentation is that one of the dangers of incantation is that it may conceal choices that have to be made, or obscure the fact that there are still a great many loose ends around. In Europe at least there remains much doubt about what the Maritime Strategy actually means. Does it mean horizontal escalation, chasing Soviet submarines under the Arctic ice, maintaining a permanent presence in the Norwegian Sea, or flattening Murmansk – or all of them? The Maritime Strategy remains at the level of broad generalities because it is not intended to be the kind of 'campaign analysis' which actually shows what terms like 'sea control' might mean in this area.

Forward Operations would certainly be dangerous intellectually if it encouraged the idea that there is a single solution to the problems of the Far North. NATO and the United States will certainly need to develop more than one campaign option. These campaign analyses tend to show how important it is to retain control of the airfields of Northern Norway, and to make sure that the Flank is not turned in Jutland. Sustaining the campaign would be very difficult should either of those eventualities occur. If, for example, the airfields were used by the Soviet Union, Soviet aircraft would be in a position to threaten aircraft from bases in Britain going to the Central Front (about one-third of the total) and would make NATO's control of the North Atlantic much more difficult. Carriers could be very important in a situation like this.

One such option might be to try to draw the Soviet maritime strike aircraft in a kind of rerun of the Battle of the Philippine Sea in 1944. Probably the critical consideration as to whether it would be done or not would be a judgement about the level of air control required for some operation up there. It would really be scenario-driven, and not fought just for the hell of it.

The second lesson revealed by campaign analysis is the importance of the Baltic area to the outcome of events in the whole of the Northern Flank, and indeed to those of the Central Front as well. Controlling Denmark would allow the Soviet Union to encircle Scandinavia, bring Britain directly into the firing line and enable the Soviet Navy to sustain a long campaign by the resulting capacity to use the dockyards of the Baltic. But there is a problem here in that the NATO tendency to compartmentalize its area of responsibility into discrete regions and not relate them very much to each other tends to conceal the need to work out priorities. It may therefore be that naval planners considering the problems of one area may find that some of the runners do not turn up on the day of the race because they are away somewhere else. This could happen in the Baltic Approaches, or in Northern Norway for that matter. What, for example, if things go well off Northern Norway, but badly in Jutland, or the other way about?

Part V
The Land Campaign

11 Land–Air Operations in the North
Major General Sir Jeremy Moore, KCB, OBE, MC

This chapter is not the product of someone from an academic or research establishment, or indeed from Whitehall. But where perhaps my background may help me make some useful comment is that for five of my last six years in the service I was responsible for the preparation of forces to fight precisely the battle we are addressing and for the other year, as is all too well known, I was privileged to play a part in an operation which had at least sufficient features in common with some of those which any future campaign on the Northern Flank would face to be worth consideration. Though I shall allude to the air battle and to some of its effects, I shall not attempt to deal with it fully, leaving that to Air Vice-Marshal Price in Chapter 12.

I have therefore as it were surveyed my experience as a land forces commander and land deputy to identify shafts of light which will I hope help to illuminate the scene. The result is more a dappled woodland glade than a 'broad sunlit upland', to use the Churchillian phrase. What I think is interesting is to see whether the individual shafts come together to give us overall patterns. I think in some cases they do. Nevertheless, to continue the woodland metaphor, I am not trying to delineate the wood; I am examining some of the trees.

The strongest shafts of light which have illuminated my thinking have, it seems to me, emanated from three principal directions. The first of these, and I quite deliberately put it first rather than in its usual position at the end of most military appreciations or papers, is logistics.

Logistics have so often turned out to be the *sine qua non* upon which all action has depended, and indeed it is always a major factor in the amphibious operations with which I am particularly familiar. This was thoroughly recognized as far as the South Atlantic campaign was concerned, but I would propose to you – and will argue – that it will be just as overriding a factor in any future campaign which might be conducted in the Northern European Command. Its rightful place in military affairs is indeed as the servant of the operational side, but if we do not order our logistic affairs with great forethought, no amount of effort or material at the time will prevent operations grinding to a halt.

Trying to find a suitable title for my second subject has given me some difficulty. It cannot quite be called 'command', though it has to do with that subject, nor can I describe it as 'tactics', for it is more than that. Let me call it the 'conduct of operations', for we know that the Soviets give great weight to this in their thinking, and that for instance they have in all probability arranged the boundaries of the responsibilities of their commanders to give them, as they perceive it, a considerable advantage, and that by having a developed tactical doctrine at a level which we do not – 'operational' is I understand the correct translation of their word for it – they also believe they have the edge on us in this important field.

The third subject I shall address is quality. By this I do not just mean that it is easier to win if your people and equipment have better performance parameters and are more reliable than those of the enemy. I do to a degree mean that, but not I think just in the simplistic sense, as I shall again try to argue.

I would like to begin with an observation upon the strategic scene. I have noted how both the Soviet and the Western need to fight the Northern battle have shifted, withdrawn and advanced over the years; in particular, how the balance of interest in the defence of Northern Norway, in the earlier years following the formation of the Northern European Command, moved from the sea to the land–air battle, because of the lack of Soviet naval strength. And now of course the Gorshkov years have changed things again, and we have come full cycle and see, with the articulation of the United States Maritime Strategy, the revival of the idea that this particular theatre is a maritime one.

Personally, I have long viewed North Norway, with its lacey pattern of fjords and islands, as 'fringe upon a petticoat' (if I may misborrow from Rosalind), but I have always seen the petticoat as the Norwegian Sea rather than continental Europe. This may seem a familiar theme, but I make no apology for reiterating it, because some of what I say later will relate to it. I was attracted, in this context, by Colonel Alford's description in Chapter 6 of a circular problem, when he suggested his syllogism: 'who controls the Norwegian Sea depends on who controls the North Norwegian airfields; who controls those airfields depends on who gets there first; and who gets there first depends on who controls the Norwegian Sea'. I shall come back to these circular arguments later; I would like merely to note at this stage that while the balance favours us because we – in the shape of the

Norwegians alone for most of the year – are more 'there now' than our potential adversary, he has the potential to reverse that and achieve surprise by choosing the moment when it comes to the point.

I must also make the point, because I think it may not be fully apparent in the limited space available in this chapter, that I too acknowledge the Northern Flank as having the meaning assigned to it by NATO, covering the Northern European Command based in Oslo, with its three subordinate commands of North and South Norway and the Baltic Approaches. Often, however, the problems are particularly highlighted in one area, and certainly the climatic demands upon training have ensured that I have given more of my time to one of them than the other two.

Perhaps this is also the right point at which to express my agreement with another point made by Colonel Alford. This is that provided the Danes do not hand Zealand over on a plate by diverting too many of their forces to the defence of the mainland, and provided we continue to conduct regular and serious training to exercise the Allied reinforcement of the local forces, the greatest threat to the Baltic Approaches region territorially would come from an attack through Schleswig-Holstein, across the Kiel Canal and would aim to occupy Jutland and its airfields. This will not be an easy threat to meet, particularly if the Allied air forces have a hard time keeping the air sufficiently clear to cover the deployment and logistic maintenance of the reinforcement formations which will be needed to back the German and Danish forces in place there. The point is also perhaps worth making that, as I shall argue is the case in the far North too, this Allied ability to reinforce and maintain its forces will be very much more difficult to interdict if it, or at least part of it, is based upon a real amphibious capability. It should not rely entirely upon the limited port and airfield facilities, which are particularly vulnerable – and, in the latter case, likely to be more than fully occupied with the air battle.

Now, having alluded to the conditions in Denmark, I want to remind us all about the North of Norway; that is to say the three northern counties of Finnmark, Troms and Nordland. We have all no doubt read it all before, but some of it bears repeating. Troms is the tactical core of this area and has to be the essential objective of any Soviet attack in the region, for I am sure they do not forget the effect the Germans were able to have upon their own resupply line from Scotland in the Second World War, making use of the airfields and harbours there. It is here, westwards and southwards from Lyngenfjord and Skibotn, with the Finnish Wedge pointing its finger down to the sea, that the all-important ground lies. High desolate fjelle rise sharply from the fjord edges and the narrow valley floors to 1000 m and more. There are long, long fjords and a mass of islands and leads (Norway has 13 000 miles of coast and 150 000 islands). The rocky uneven ground is impracticable for most off-the-road movement by vehicles whether under deep snow in winter or alternating rock and marsh in summer. As was tragically demonstrated in 1986 there is a severe risk of avalanches. This is an area the size of the Benelux countries with a population of but half a million and only the infrastructure to support that. The famous E6, for instance, is not even 'made up' throughout the whole of this vital area, and it is in places only one track wide. It is nevertheless often the only route for anyone relying upon wheeled transport, though its capacity is so clearly greatly less than even one major road in Central Europe. The railway, too, is single track, and anyway finishes at Bödö – a long way further South.

It is at the north-eastern end of this area – around Skibotn – that the Commander North Norway must begin to fight his main land battle. His small forward detachments and delaying forces will no doubt have imposed *materiel* and time penalties upon the 45th Motor Rifle Division before it reaches this area. The Finnmarks ridge is not suited to a protracted defence, and though its loss will leave the enemy in possession of Alta and Banak it will not uncover the core airfields at Bardufoss, Evenes and Andoya (and to a lesser extent Tromso), nor the ports of Harstad, Narvik and Tromso. And let us remember that two of these airfields, as well as two of the ports, are on islands.

We thus come to a consideration of the logistic problem. In the Falklands, we had to maintain seven battalions with limited artillery support, virtually no armour and little vehicular transport. We were fighting against a static enemy, with equally limited artillery, and no apparent inclination to make rigorous attacks upon us. Our requirements for defensive fire tasks were minimal and yet we needed to move artillery ammunition forward as I recall it at a rate of some 500 tons a day. It is not difficult to visualize that the E6, even if it can be kept fully open in the face of attacks from the air or the sea, or indeed the ground, will be fully occupied with the maintenance of Brigade North and the reinforcement regiments the Norwegians plan to deploy, let alone Allied forces. Furthermore, the ports and airfields themselves have only a limited capacity. From San Carlos to Mount Kent was about 65 helicopter km, from Harstad or Evenes to this battle zone is some 160. And again the airfields, like those in Jutland, are likely to find themselves extremely busy with the air defence battle.

There is also the matter of vulnerability. The entry points and the roads are well known and are readily accessible to attack from the air as well as from the sea. In the South Atlantic, again, we found that our main logistic base in Ajax Bay, despite the air defence forces on land and at sea around it, was very vulnerable. So, as was demonstrated in one case, were the harbors at Teal Inlet and Port Pleasant where the two brigades established their forward resupply facilities. And perhaps I should make the point that despite the psychological effect of the loss of two companies in one fell swoop, it was largely because of the logistic problems that our initial reaction to the Argentine air attack of 8 June was that it would delay our administrative preparation for the main battle by some four days. In the event, we were able to recover two of those days, but we were not interfered with again.

I am well aware of the danger of learning false lessons from events like this, such as the preposterous suggestions I have heard that because we managed to make do without something on that occasion we would not need it in future – Airborne Early Warning, a remotely-piloted reconnaissance vehicle, or a large enough deck to mount properly co-ordinated tactical helicopter landings occur to me. The age and lack of sophistication of the Argentine aircraft are I think well known, though I suspect that at times this was not entirely a disadvantage to them. The forward supply area at Port Pleasant was attacked, though it was very nearly missed despite being visible from enemy ground positions. That at Teal Inlet, although it was in position for much longer, was never attacked, I suspect never discovered.

The point of all this, of course, is that what will give formations in North Norway (or indeed in many parts of the Baltic Approaches or South Norway) the ability to sustain themselves logistically, is a retained amphibious capability. Dispersed stocks, away from the obvious areas, concealed around some of the many suitable settlements, inlets and fjordside beaches will be extremely difficult to find in fast modern aircraft, and with an amphibious forces capability for crossing and recrossing coastlines will be relatively flexible in distribution. A system which is independent of the roads will ensure that the enemy will find locations very hard to predict, and therefore much more problem to discover, let alone attack.

Now I would like to move on to this question of the conduct of operations, so let us start with some of the Soviet thinking. It has been suggested that the Soviet intention would be to put the North Norwegian airfields out of action for the duration of the battle of the Norwegian Sea, and that would certainly seem a sensible aim for them.

However, my experience makes me doubt whether by air attack, by missile strike (assuming of course we rule out nuclear or chemical weapons), by raiding from the sea or by bombardment it would be possible to keep those airfields out of action. Put them out for a while, certainly, but surely not keeping them out for the duration of the battle of the Norwegian Sea. An airman's comments on this would be interesting.

My second point here is to comment upon the Soviet employment of *desant* operations to ease the path of their normal mechanized formations carrying out the main thrust, for which of course they have in Leningrad Military District (LEMD) the Pechenga-based 63rd Naval Infantry Brigade, and the 76th Guards Airborne Division. It is interesting to note that, though in 1940 the Germans made six landings along almost three-quarters of the length of the Norwegian coast, and thus achieved just the sort of strategic surprise which is such an important feature of Warsaw Pact thinking, the Soviets themselves made only a number of short-range naval infantry assaults in support of their attack on the German 19th Mountain Infantry Corps in October 1944. It has been suggested that they might attempt such a long-range operation as the Germans did if they thought they could achieve almost complete strategic surprise. I do not believe this is at all likely, partly because the Norwegians are so clearly better prepared than in 1940 and fully alert to such a danger, partly because I do not think they would regard the forces they have immediately available to them for such an operation as anything like adequate, and partly because it would be other factors in other areas which would dictate the timing anyway.

It seems to me most likely that amphibious landings would be used, in close support of conventional ground moves, to ease the task of the latter by cutting off defending Norwegian (and later Allied) units, and thus preventing the orderly, steady fighting withdrawal which the Soviet commander would find least to his liking. This, I believe, would give us an opportunity to exploit a more flexible use of amphibious capabilities, both to cut his resupply to his main force and to ensure that our own units in contact are not 'cut off' just because the enemy is sitting astride a road. In such fluid situations who is cut off and who is not can be made largely a matter of mental atttiude. The recent Sandhurst Soviet Studies Research Centre booklet on Soviet amphibious warfare makes the point that 'during the whole of the [Second World War], the logistical system for supporting Soviet amphibious landings was never properly organized and the principles were not properly established', and concludes that this failure still shapes the concept of their use today.[1] Nothing in any recent Soviet works on amphibious assaults suggests a departure from the principle of using them simply as a flank unit to the main front.

Much, too, is made of the Soviet doctrine of exploiting the weaknesses of an opponent's command structure. The obvious and simple example is the way they seek to establish the location of boundaries between armies – especially those of different nations – and then direct their thrust, under a single command, along this axis. In the North I believe it is worth looking at the relationship between the naval and land forces on both sides, to ensure that we have a really unified structure which reduces weaknesses on our side and exploits them on theirs. Here, of course, I refer to the essential nature of the Northern theatre as being a maritime one. It seems to me that, whatever the politics of the Alliance – and I do not wish to suggest these are of no importance – for the most efficient execution in war the command in NEC ought to be maritime. Although the Soviet need to fight the war in North Norway is the result of his need to fight the fleet battle as far South in the Norwegian Sea as possible, I believe his essentially land-orientated tactical thinking must give us fertile ground for exploitation. In other words, if our opponent is thinking essentially 'land' and we are thinking essentially 'maritime', I believe we will have got it right.

Quite a bit of what I have already said has had to do with quality. You will not be surprised to hear from someone with a background in my Corps that I am wholly convinced of the value of mottoes like 'Train hard, fight easy', and of course I have had the opportunity to observe how much the expenditure of sweat in peacetime saves blood in wartime, though I recognize that that is very much an infantryman's way of putting things. But I have also observed that the ability to perform efficiently and economically is not associated only with the expenditure of energy. It has also to do with a retained ability to practice the art. Making do with less than the ideal has worked, time and again because there have been people present who have the experience to know the snags, because they have done it before, and who know what they are trying to achieve because they have done it with the right equipment. I take leave to doubt very strongly whether we would have been able successfully to mount the operation in the South Atlantic in 1982, which employed so many ships taken up from trade in the amphibious role, had we not had a substantial body of experience within the Naval Service in the operation of amphibious ships; and this of course we had, and will only have, so long as we retain an amphibious warfare squadron in full-time service. This is, of course, part of the case that such ships converted from civilian uses are force multipliers and not substitutes for the core capability.

While on this subject of quality and commitment, it is also perhaps interesting to note than the UK has come to committing her amphibious capability more and more to the defence of the Northern region at least partly as a result of a perceived waning of the requirement elsewhere – though 1982 provided perhaps a timely reminder that such requirements have not necessarily entirely disappeared. Marines are not intrinsically any more suitable to train for cold weather operations, nor even perhaps mountain operations, than any other high-quality flexibly-minded corps, though it is a form of warfare which demands continued and repeated attention if, in winter anyway, troops are to have any time left over from surviving the climate to fight, let alone take advantage of the environment. They are, however, just what is needed to fight on Europe's Arctic Flank because they are marines, because at the lower level they are used to understanding sea coasts and using waterborne assets to enhance their landfighting capabilities, while at the higher level they have a maritime background.

In any future war on land on the Norwegian Flank the enemy will undoubtedly have the advantage of numbers and weight of materiel, but we can have the countervailing advantage of quality. In equipment terms, this means in performance, but more more importantly it means in reliability; in tactical and strategic terms, it means in thinking out the operating techniques and methods to exploit his weaknesses and difficulties while taking advantage of our own strengths; and in people terms, it means preparing ourselves physically and mentally to exploit our local knowledge, and a superior set of command arrangements.

I have explained some of the ways in which I believe we can win this land battle. I have said that in my view to concentrate and support our formations effectively and flexibly depends upon an amphibious capability; to gain the tactical advantage depends upon an amphibious capability; to cope with the enemy doctrine depends upon an amphibious capability; and to divert Soviet attention by threatening his base depends upon an amphibious capability.

I would now like to suggest another way of looking at the circular arguments put before you in Chapter 6. The freedom of the Fleet to operate in the Norwegian Sea depends upon who holds the North Norwegian airfields; who holds the North Norwegian airfields depends upon who can sustain the necessary land forces to do so; who can sustain the necessary land forces to hold the airfields depends upon who can operate his fleet freely in the Norwegian Sea. The one most likely to succeed in this is the one who best understands this essentially maritime problem. In the Soviet Studies Research Centre booklet I have already mentioned (p. 136), the chapter on the Soviet strategic view of conflict on this flank concludes by wondering whether the two Soviet Motor Rifle Divisions and ancillary forces at present stationed in the LEMD are capable of invading North Norway without reinforcement, as some say that they are: 'If they are', it suggests, 'Norway is under a greater threat than the rest of us; if they are not, the Norwegians can sleep as soundly as anyone else'.[2] I think my conclusion must be that the Norwegians can indeed sleep as soundly as anyone else – provided that neither they nor we do!

Notes

1. C. N. Donnelly *et al.*, *Soviet Amphibious Operations: Implications for the Security of NATO's Northern Flank* (Sandhurst: Soviet Studies Centre, 1985) pp. 53–60.
2. Donnelly *et al.*, *Soviet Amphibious Operations*, p. 16.

12 The Northern Flank: The Air Dimension
Air Vice-Marshal John Price, CBE (Rtd)

I have been asked to comment, from an airman's point of view, upon land–air operations on the Northern Flank. I shall not go into minor 'tactics'; my intention is rather to draw out a few major points, in the course of which specific air points will naturally emerge.

General Moore has stated in Chapter 11 that he would look at a few trees rather than the wood, and I also believe that we must look at the Northern Flank as all of one piece. And we must set it in the wider landscape of the defence of Europe. The maritime aspects of operations in the North are indeed important: they provide one of the elements in the layered defence of the North American reinforcement sea lanes to Europe, and may also contribute directly to the land–air battle. But that is not the full story, however strongly argued in this volume (Chapters 7–10) and elsewhere.

Looking at the matter in the round, and nowadays at some professional distance, it seems to me most unlikely that the Soviets would choose to fight NATO by way of an offensive against Northern Norway alone. As Dr Wood stated in Chapter 7, the Soviets are not adventurist. The potential risks would seem to be out of all proportion to any possible gain provided, of course, that NATO continues to demonstrate its cohesion as an Alliance – and how this might be done in the North is a point to which I will attend later. The Soviets would surely be most likely to fight in Northern Norway as a supporting action to their operations in the Central Region – and in ways which would not jeopardize those operations.

But as a defensive Alliance, NATO's first aim must be to deter (see Tables 12.1, 12.2 and Figure 12.1) – to show that gains and risks do not balance; to show that the Alliance has the will, intention and capability to reinforce lightly-defended areas which might be threatened. How is this will, intention and capability to be demonstrated? The question of 'will' must be left to our political masters; intention and capability are more in the domain of the military and can be demonstrated by possession of the ability to reinforce quickly, and the regular exercise

Table 12.1 Allied Forces, Northern Europe

1. *Introduction*
   The Headquarters Allied Forces Northern Europe (AFNORTH) was established in 1951 and (as shown by Figure 12.1) is one of 4 subordinate commands accountable to Supreme Allied Commander Europe (SACEUR). The Headquarters, AFNORTH, is currently based at Kolsaas (9 miles west of Oslo) and the appointment is held by a UK 4-star General.
2. *Area of Responsibility*
   AFNORTH's area of responsibility comprises Norway, Denmark, Federal Republic of Germany north of the Elbe river, and adjacent sea areas. Collectively, this is known as the Northern European Command (NEC). The NEC is then divided into 3 tactically separate but interdependent areas: North Norway, South Norway and the Baltic Approaches (again shown by Figure 12.1).
3. *Divisions within the Northern European Command*
   The Northern European Command is divided up as follows:
   a. *Commander Allied Forces South Norway (COMSONOR)* has HQ located at Oslo. His mission is threefold: defend the Command area, reinforce Allied Forces North Norway and receive and employ external reinforcements.
   b. *Commander Allied Forces North Norway (COMNON)* has HQ located at Reitan, near Bödö and is manned by all Norwegian personnel. COMNON's responsibility is to ensure the defence of ACE's Northern region.
   c. *Commander Allied Forces Baltic Approaches (COMBALTAP)* has HQ located at Karup, Denmark. In peacetime, COMBALTAP's mission is to carry out the planning, co-ordination and training of the wartime operations of the Danish and German forces.

Source: MOD.

Table 12.2 The Northern Region of ACE

Land reinforcements
1. *ACE Mobile Force (AMF)* This is a multi-national, brigade-sized force combined with a number of air Squadrons which is intended for rapid deployment early in a period of tension to demonstrate NATO solidarity (and, if necessary, to fight alongside theatre troops). It has several deployments options, two of which are in the Northern Region, so its presence on the Northern Flank cannot be guaranteed.
2. *Second Marine Amphibious Force (II MAF)* The United States provides II MAF for the defense of the Northern Region. This divisional size force firstly deploys 4 MAB, a brigade-sized force with integral air support, to North Norway and then follows with the remainder staging through the UK to the area within the Region which is most in need of support.
3. *Canadian Air–Sea Transported Brigade Group (CAST)* The CAST is a light brigade group which is dedicated to the defense of North Norway. It is moved partly by air and partly by sea.

Table 12.2   The Northern Region of ACE – *continued*

4. *The UK/NL Amphibious Force (UK/NL AF)* This mainly regular brigade-sized force comprises of 3 British and 1 Dutch battalion equivalents with organic combat, helicopter and logistic support. It is assigned to SACLANT who has agreed with SACEUR that the force may be employed in support of the Northern Region to make best use of its Mountain and Arctic Warfare capability.
5. *United Kingdom Mobile Force (UKMF)* This brigade-sized force has deployment options in Zealand and Schleswig-Holstein. It consists of 4 infantry battalions with armoured reconnaissance, medium artillery, engineer and a large logistic support group.
6. *SACEUR's Strategic Reserve Land (SSR(L))* The United States Ninth Infantry Division is a modern, well-equipped force which has options for deployment in the Northern Region. It is retained in the UK for use by SACEUR as part of his land reserves. All or part of the remainder of the SSR(L) could be deployed to the Northern Region.

Air reinforcements
7. *Regional Air Reinforcements* 6 Squadrons, one of which is British, reinforce Norway and up to 7 Squadrons, 2 of which are British, reinforce Denmark. The 3 British Squadrons are all Jaguars.
8. *SACEUR's Strategic Reserves Air (SSR(A))* 12 Squadrons, which includes 3 UK Tornado and 1 UK Harrier Squadrons, are retained in UK for use by SACEUR. All or part of this force could be available in the Northern Region.

Source: MOD.

of that ability. The Alliance's cohesion is thus also demonstrated. In the case of Northern Norway the reinforcements in earnest would consist not just of the UK/NL Command Brigade; important and useful though that will be, it must be seen in the context of about six regular Norwegian Brigades which would be likely to precede it into position, and of the American and Canadian Brigades which will follow. Equally, it must be seen in the light of the major air reinforcements which will flow in even faster from South Norway, the United Kingdom and North America, in the first hours and days.

This point about early arrival – timeliness, in other words – seems critical to me as providing not only an early warning signal to a potential enemy of our firm intention, but also as a way of raising the stakes rapidly. Firm possession of the airfields at the earliest moment would be a major achievement. In the Falklands context, one would have secured possession of the Mount Pleasant airfield in March 1982; and that is worth a thought. These air reinforcements, and reinforcements brought in by air, will be the foundation of North

143

```
                    SUPREME ALLIED COMMANDER EUROPE
                              (SACEUR)
                     Shape                        Belguim
                     Casteau

                    DEPUTY SUPREME ALLIED COMMANDERS EUROPE
```

| COMMANDER-IN-CHIEF ALLIED FORCES NORTHERN EUROPE (CINCNORTH) — Kolsas, Norway | COMMANDER-IN-CHIEF ALLIED FORCES CENTRAL EUROPE — Brunssum, Netherlands | COMMANDER-IN-CHIEF ALLIED FORCES SOUTHERN EUROPE — Naples, Italy | COMMANDER UNITED KINGDOM AIR FORCES — High Wycombe, UK |

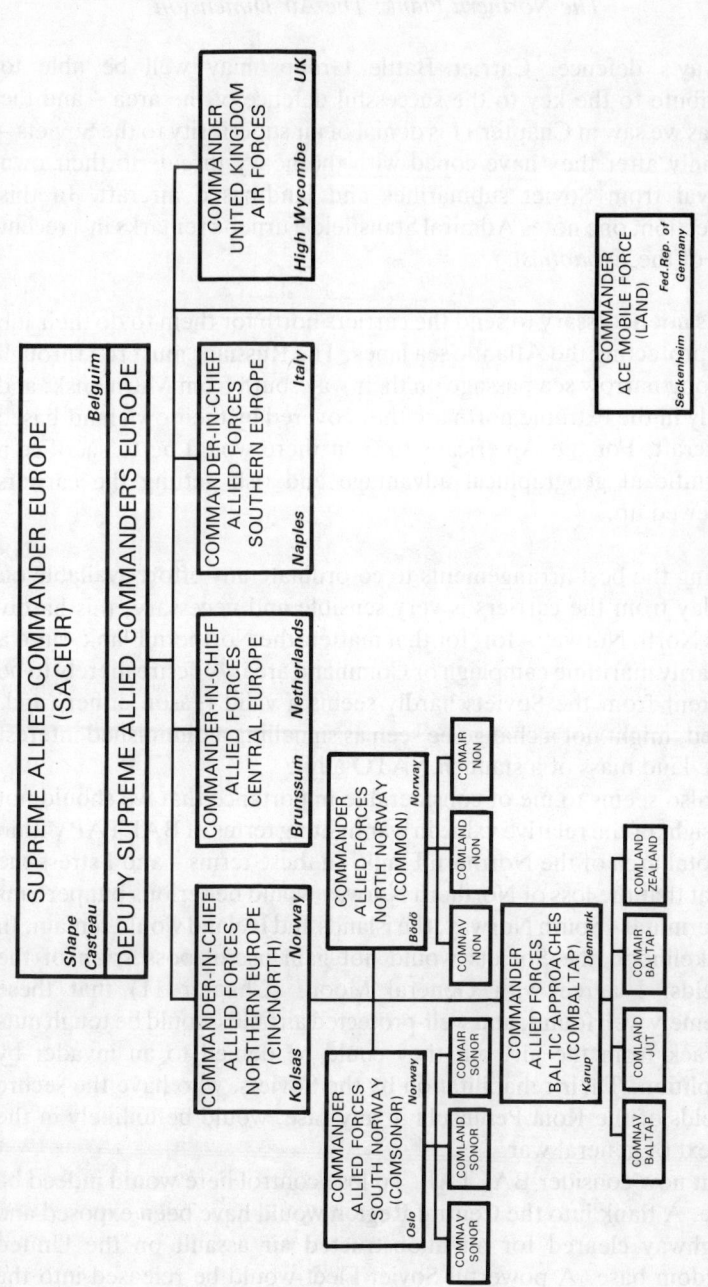

COMMANDER ACE MOBILE FORCE (LAND) — Seckenheim, Fed. Rep. of Germany

Under CINCNORTH:

- COMMANDER ALLIED FORCES SOUTH NORWAY (COMSONOR) — Oslo, Norway
  - COMNAV SONOR
  - COMLAND SONOR
  - COMAIR SONOR
- COMMANDER ALLIED FORCES NORTH NORWAY (COMNON) — Bödö, Norway
  - COMNAV NON
  - COMLAND NON
  - COMAIR NON
- COMMANDER ALLIED FORCES BALTIC APPROACHES (COMBALTAP) — Karup, Denmark
  - COMNAV BALTAP
  - COMLAND JUT
  - COMAIR BALTAP
  - COMLAND ZEALAND

Figure 12.1 Position of Commander-in-Chief, Allied Forces Northern Europe, in Allied Command Europe

Norway's defence. Carrier Battle Groups may well be able to contribute to the key to the successful defence of the area – and the key, as we saw in Chapter 11 is denial of air superiority to the Soviets – but only after they have coped with the heavy threats to their own survival from Soviet submarines and land-based aircraft. In this connection, one notes Admiral Stansfield Turner's remarks in a recent issue of the *Economist*:

> it is not necessary to send the carriers north for them to do their job of protecting the Atlantic sea lanes. The Russians must run through a long narrow sea passage on their way south from Murmansk, and only in the extreme north are they covered by their own land-based aircraft. For the Americans to fight there would be to sacrifice a significant geographical advantage and risk getting the carriers chewed up.[1]

Making the best arrangements to co-ordinate any effort available on the day from the carriers is very sensible and necessary; this hardly turns North Norway – for, for that matter, the Northern Flank – into a primarily maritime campaign or Command area. A desire merely to be different from the Soviets hardly seems a valid reason either (and, indeed, might not a change be seen as signalling a diminished interest in the land mass of a staunch NATO ally)?

It also seems to me of considerable importance that we should not lose sight of the relative value in war fighting terms of BALTAP within the total area of the Northern Flank. In these terms – and I stress the caveat that the loss of Northern Norway would be serious but perhaps not terminal – South Norway, the islands and Iceland would remain. In all likelihood the Soviets would not gain useful possession of the airfields; I agree with General Moore (Chapter 11) that these extremely well found, and well-protected airfields would be tough nuts to crack from the air, but they could be denied to an invader by demolition. Their rehabilitation by the Soviets, who have the secure airfields of the Kola Peninsula in any case, would be unlikely in the context of general war.

But now consider BALTAP. To lose control here would indeed be grave. A flank into the Central Region would have been exposed and a highway cleared for an unobstructed air assault on the United Kingdom base. A powerful Soviet Fleet would be released into the Shallow Seas. General Moore may be right and land attacks into Jutland would be mounted from Germany. But even before that, with

BALTAP air defences beaten down, Warsaw Pact air power could be easing the land advance into Germany.

When one quietly considers all this, it seems to me that in these days of limited defence budgets the Alliance in general, and the United Kingdom in particular, has struck about the right balance when allocating resources and forces between and within the NATO commands. I would strongly contest any contention that the UK has become a flank nation. My consideration of the military history of the Northern Flank reminded me of the dominant position by air power during operations in 1940. The characteristics of air power then displayed – swift reaction, flexibility, ubiquity – seem no less important on the Northern Flank today. We need to train, think and plan for land–air operations so that no-one in the future will be able to write, as Churchill did:

> We, who had command of the sea and could pounce anywhere on an undefended coast, were outpaced by the enemy moving by land across very large distances in the face of every obstacle.[2]

Notes

1. The *Economist*, 19 April 1986, p. 50.
2. W. S. Churchill, *The Gathering Storm* (London: Cassell, 1984) p. 571.

13 The Military Importance of the Northern Flank: A Dutch View
Major-General A. C. Lamers RNLMC (Rtd)

Discussing the military importance of the Northern Flank I would like to confine myself to the territory of Norway and the contiguous sea areas. From a command point of view, Denmark and the Baltic Approaches belong to NATO's North, but geographically and strategically they are clearly a part of the Central Sector. It is impossible to reduce both areas to the same strategic denominator; obviously the geographic situation and the configuration of Norway give it a very special strategic significance with regard to the Barents Sea, the Norwegian Sea, the GIUK Gap, the North Sea and the Baltic Approaches. It is important, then, since it provides outlets to the ocean and vital SLOCs, as well as to important concentration and deployment areas of naval forces. And it is also a fact that Norway is within striking distance of all the countries around the North Sea, that is of NATO's heartland.

Norwegian terrain and climate make special demands upon (and set limitations to) the forces that wish to operate in that area. This is a country for light and relatively small formations. They need to be specially trained, experienced, hardened and well acquainted with the area, in order to master the extremes of climate and terrain. There are only very limited possibilities for the movement and deployment of large armoured and motorized formations. Those who, in this pre-eminently littoral area, can make the most of the sea to move their military forces and to project their power ashore have an undeniable advantage.

Norway's rather obvious isolation is another essential characteristic of the Flank. From whatever angle we look at the Northern Flank, from the west or from the east, it is not connected to the Centre; the relation between the Flank and the Centre to which it apparently belongs is an indirect one. The consequences of operations on the Flank will not immediately affect the situation or the course of things in the Centre; but their long-term effects can be very significant indeed.

If the Warsaw Pact tried to decide a conflict with the West by a gigantic armoured sweep to the Atlantic Ocean, as a way of seizing this continent within the shortest time, and before a substantial reaction from the United States comes into effect, what would they have in mind for the Northern Flank? The prospect of the conquest of Norway would undoubtedly cause them problems because it would be almost impossible for them to bring their superiority in manpower, armour and heavy combat support into play. NATO ground forces, which they would not be able to avoid, are probably better than anywhere else prepared for and familiar with their task. It is almost certain that Soviet forces would be confronted with superior NATO naval forces and very strong airforces; all this would make their prospects for victory seem dim.

In short, they will be faced with a job for which their opponents might hold the winning cards. If Norwegian territory after the Soviet opening offensive for the larger part remains in NATO hands (the loss of Finnmark and Troms might be difficult to prevent) a situation would develop which could be very precarious for the Russians. The presence of a strong enemy bastion on the Flank and in the rear of what by that time possibly would be a Soviet continent would be dangerous for them since it might dominate vital lines of communication, but also could function as a jumping-off board for NATO counter-actions. At the very least the prospect of all this would tie strong Warsaw Pact forces to Denmark and Northern Germany. But there will be more for them to worry about. Even if the struggle for Norway were decided in the Warsaw Pact's favour, they will have to pay for it with a considerable loss, especially in naval and air forces. Now these are exactly the forces they will need urgently to complete the conquest of Europe, for example in a final assault on the British Isles. To sum up, a Soviet attack on Norway would run serious risk of a grave loss in military strength and time while the odds are that vital territory would remain in NATO hands.

It is easy to be too optimistic, however. Norway's natural and structural strategic strength has to be secured to our advantage, and how sure are we of our ground? For the defence of Norway is not based on ready military forces; instead, its actual and ultimately considerable strength depends very much on a fast and unhindered mobilization of the Norwegian forces and on the fast reinforcement of her allies. Bearing all this in mind, the time taken to complete the mobilization and to bring in a substantial part of the dedicated reinforcements would be a matter of risk. Is there not the possibility of surprise attack – that is to say, one that directs itself with all possible surprise simultaneously on a number of targets spread out all over the country? Such an attack could lead to the disruption of the mobilization and the planned deployment of the Norwegian forces, and might put the Soviets in possession of key harbours and airfields by which they could prevent or seriously hinder the entry of Allied reinforcements and so give them a position from which they could make a NATO counter-attack a very hazardous enterprise. All these things considered, it may be wondered seriously what respect the aggressors would have for the neutral countries in that area; bearing this in mind, it is amazing that so little attention is given to the April 1940 scenario.

We tend to project the expected Soviet attack and the NATO counter-measures along a North–South axis. The build-up of NATO forces goes almost exactly along this line, and so does the sequence of their mobilization or their arrival from abroad. Moreover, the majority of the Allied reinforcements, however 'high performance' they may be, depend for their entry into the country on availability of airfields. Their arrival points are fixed and static, with all the inherent disadvantages that this brings. The best entry possibilities are those of the UK/NL Landing Force (UK/NL LF). They enjoy a great freedom in choosing their landing point and their descent should in most cases be an unpleasant surprise to the enemy. Unfortunately the UK/NL LF is not a very strong one when it comes to assault capacity, and this seriously curtails the possibilities of its excellent landing force. Nevertheless I think that this unit will be constant source of special anxiety to the Russians.

The Dutch contribution to the UK/NL LF comprises:

1. The 1st and 2nd Amphibious Combat Groups which are battalion-sized formations; the first only is fully trained for Arctic operations.
2. The Whisky company which is a part of 45 Commando Royal Marines.
3. A landing craft assault detachment and a Special Boat Section (SBS) which are also both fully integrated into Royal Marine organizations.

The surveillance, control and defence of such a long, irregular and often deeply-cut coast like that of Norway is in fact an almost impossible job. Only in the presence of the direct threat of strong NATO naval forces do we have reasonable guarantees for a reliable defence; these forces are important because they create serious risks for the Soviets which might influence their plans in our favour.

Such naval forces need a strong air component as well as an amphibious assault capacity. I would agree with those (see Chapters 1–10) who are critical of the fixation of the Atlantic maritime defence on the GIUK Gap and who are instead in favour of a strong naval presence in the Norwegian Sea with significant offensive potential. I do think that the security of the Northern Flank ultimately depends on it, and that in turn will give us essential assets we need in any confrontation with the Warsaw Pact.

There was a time that the high North had a much more low-key position in the political and military field of tension, as a place probably mainly for crisis prevention and limited conflicts. But the area above the Arctic circle is now associated with such important strategic aspects as:

1. The SSBN bastion in the Arctic Sea.
2. The Soviet intention to maintain a global naval presence.
3. The development of a most powerful military potential on the Kola Peninsula.

The possibility of isolated provocative, small-scale military activities seems now to be much less. They would cause too many drawbacks for the Soviets, mainly because they might disturb the Nordic Balance in favour of NATO.

These are reasonable considerations, but the question is whether they are reasonable enough to exclude the possibility of a limited threat to the Northern Flank. We should not think of an attack on the Northern Flank only in the context of a general assault on Western Europe, but also as possible area for local conflict. After all it is up to the Russians to weigh the pros and cons of crisis provocation. If at any time it suits their policy to challenge NATO in the low-tension field, I think we have to reckon with the North as a probable place of action. This would require our responding immediately and effectively with a force which has the strength and flexibility to meet any contingency, preferably without an unnecessary and threatening build up of counter-forces; an always ready and balanced maritime force will serve our purpose best.

Let me add that crisis management with the clear intention to prevent war was the most popular political argument in the Netherlands for participation in the defence of the Northern Flank, because here was a military effort which seemed morally acceptable. Later on, people in the Netherlands began to realize also that Norway (due to her limited human resources) would be unable to defend her vast territory, and that it would only be right for her to expect support from her NATO allies. But it is not generally accepted (either politically or militarily) that the defence of Norway is also of vital interest to the security of the Netherlands. One has to accept the fact that in a war with the Warsaw Pact the direct threat to the Netherlands comes across the North German plain. Politics and public opinion accept that that is where there is the highest priority for defence; accordingly, the Netherlands spends roughly 70 per cent of the defence budget on this.

As a traditional maritime nation, well aware of the importance of all maritime affairs for the wellbeing and security of the country, however, the Dutch certainly have an interest in the maritime defence of NATO in general, and the Netherlands in particular; but we have to limit our ambitions, and almost all maritime effort goes into ASW, for which we have built a fleet of considerable quality. Of course, the Netherlands Navy is becoming aware of the strategic importance of the Northern Flank. We realize the grave consequences of the loss of the Norwegian Sea and Norwegian airfields especially for NATO's vitally important naval defence line along the GIUK Gap and thus for her SLOCs. As a result, the role given to the defence of the flank by the Netherlands Marines and Air Force enjoy positive political and military support and there are serious intentions to develop this support by contributions to the lift capacity of the UK/NL AF. If the importance and defence of the Northern Flank is taken seriously, the further development of balanced naval forces – especially by the countries on the spot – should be considered positively.

14 The Security of the Northern Flank: A Danish View

B. Fr. Lindhardt

A SHORT SURVEY OF OPINIONS: CHANGES UNDER WAY?

Danish opinions about security in the Northern Flank area are very much influenced by Danish perceptions of the role and position of Denmark in geographical and foreign and domestic as well as internal political contexts. Denmark's geographical position as the pivotal link between SACLANT's main area of concern in the Norwegian Sea and the far North on one hand, and the Central Region (where the focus is concentrated on the North German Plain), on the other, presents the Danes with a Janus-like situation: they have to face two very different scenarios – the maritime – air environment in the SACLANT context, and the land–air environment of SACEUR's area of responsibility. Denmark – and BALTAP (Baltic Approaches, in the NATO acronym) – is of vital importance to both these major NATO Commanders.

Although Denmark is normally considered a Nordic country (by Danes and by foreign observers), it must be realized that when it comes to defence, Denmark is a continental nation. Even with respect to its function as the often mentioned 'cork-in-the-bottle' – the defence of the Baltic Narrows – this task is as much a land–air effort as a maritime one. Tri-service thinking, therefore, is the key to Danish military perceptions of Denmark's role in the defence of the North and the importance of the North. Defence in depth – forward naval and air defence in the Baltic – has for many years been the policy of Danish governments, both Social Democratic and Conservative/Liberal.

Since 1982–3, this consensus on forward defence has been in some jeopardy. A watershed of opinions about defence policies has divided the Social Democratic Party, and ideas of a 'defensive' defence are prominent amongst large sections of it. These ideas imply a 'non-threatening' territorial local-bound defence, and deep cuts in the naval, air, and army-manoeuvre capabilities of the Armed Forces. The various ideas about establishing a nuclear-free zone (NNFZ) in the Nordic area should be seen in the same overall context. If this were carried through, a possible consequence could be the withdrawal of the Scandinavian NATO countries from NATO's nuclear posture. Should these ideas be turned into a more concrete defence policy in the future, it could lead to changes in future Danish contribution to the defence of the North, the Baltic Straits and the Jutland Peninsula.

The dual role of the BALTAP area as a barrier and a potential staging area for operations is, *per se*, at the core of this controversy. BALTAP constitutes the best possibilities for securing South Norway (SONOR) as a base and staging area for the defence of the far North, which is in turn a necessity for the successful defence of Northern Norway. Moreover, BALTAP offers the best – indeed the only – possibility for a forward air defence of the British Isles themselves.

These important tasks, together with the commitments that come from BALTAP's being a Flank to the Central Region, necessitate a forward and in-depth defence of the area. In terms of land territory this has little depth, and it lies furthermore very close to the potential threat. The options of combining barrier-type operations (mining, anti-invasion defence, passive air defence) with counter-offensive operations (i.e., counter-air, interdiction and offensive maritime operations) are militarily and strategically sound, and must seem straightforward and attractive to commanders and decision-makers responsible for the area. The diversity of opinions of the prospective deterrent versus provocative effects of the planning of such operations, and even the possession of systems capable of accomplishing these types of operations, has produced two schools of perception of Danish defence policy: the posture of the present government – stressing the deterrent value of the established policy (which is the same as the one pursued by the former Social Democratic government) – and the opposition posture – stressing the provocative aspects and therefore advocating a more 'defensive' policy, as described above.

It may be assumed, however, that the confrontations sought by the Social Democratic Party in opposition over security policy matters might be toned down and turned into a more responsible stance should the party regain the power of government – this, of course, being dependent on the possibilities of gathering parliamentary support on these issues from the left or the centre-right.

REINFORCING BALTAP: THE NEED FOR AN ALLIED CONTRIBUTION

The strategic importance of BALTAP and its key role in the defence of NATO's Northern Flank are factors so demanding in terms of requirements for defensive efforts that indigenous Danish and German forces cannot meet them either on land or in the air. At sea, however, the combined Danish and German navies, although numerically inferior, are normally considered able to fulfil their essential sea-denial mission in the Baltic waters; the naval forces, consisting mainly of FPB (some 40 German and sixteen Danish boats, most of which are armed with Harpoon or Exocet and torpedoes), submarines (24 German, four Danish) and mine warfare ships (57 German, mainly small ships, and thirteen Danish, of which six are larger minelayers), with the addition of five Danish frigates, operate out of the bases of Copenhagen, Frederikshavn and Korsor in Denmark, and out of Kiel, Olpenitz, Murwik and Eckernforde in the Federal Republic. Their main tasks are to prevent Warsaw Pact forces from utilizing the Baltic in support of land operations on the North German Plain, to prevent invasion of the isles and shores of BALTAP and to support allied land and air operations in the area. Danish forces also have the high-priority task of securing the connection between the Island of Zealand (with the capital) and the mainland, the peninsula of Jutland.

On land, there are essentially two main issues for the forces of BALTAP – the forward defence at the inner German border, and the defence of the islands against sea- and/or air-borne invasion, should forward naval defence in the Baltic fail and should the air situation allow for such a venture on the part of the Warsaw Pact. Of these, the first task is the major one in all aspects. It is shouldered by the only binational Corps in NATO, the LANDJUT Corps, comprising the German 6th Panzer Grenadier Division and the Danish JUTLAND Division. Several other units, Danish and German, support this spearhead and secure the rear area in Schleswig-Holstein and Jutland. The two divisions are modern and relatively well-equipped with the Leopard 1 and the standard main battle tank, the Germans being in the process of replacing it with the Leopard 2.

There is, however, a deficit of great importance; namely an urgent need for a third manoeuvre element to provide a mobile reserve behind the front line divisions. It is also a problem that Danish forces will have to be deployed from their garrisons in Jutland in times of tension or crisis; there are no Danish forces stationed in Schleswig-Holstein in peacetime. Island defence is undertaken by Danish forces in the Zealand archipelago and in Bornholm.

Both naval and land operations in this triservice region are interdependent – and both are still more dependent on air forces. On the maritime side, the German Naval Air Arm is a very potent force with its Tornados possessing a most efficient striking power; the Royal Danish Air Force operates squadrons specifically trained for TASMO and specializes in anti-invasion operations in close co-operation with the Germans. Air defence is provided by Danish and German I-HAWK units and Danish air defence aircraft. A shortage in numbers increases the need for reinforcements. Counter-air operations and interdiction missions can be undertaken by Danish and some German aircraft. In this there are also requirements for external reinforcements which are especially important because of the very good opportunities offered by the facilities in Jutland and the strategic geography of the whole region. The air stations in Jutland are capable of supporting a large number of combat aircraft, and civilian installations can accommodate the associated transport and liaison aircraft. There are depots for petrol, oil and lubricants (POL) and ammunition. In all seven Danish and four German Air Force Squadrons are available.

Numerically, the Danish contribution to the defence of BALTAP comprises Army forces of roughly 87 000 men, supported by more than 60 000 Home Guard soldiers, 10 000 airmen with 12 400 Home Guard airmen, and 4700 sailors with 5200 Home Guard sailors. In Air Force and Navy, a high state of readiness is maintained but Army units rely heavily on mobilization.

In total, COMBALTAP will have at his disposal about 350 000 soldiers, sailors, and airmen – of which about 200 000 will be Danish – and roughly 220 warships, 275 combat aircraft, more than 600 main battle tanks (MBTs), and about 700 artillery pieces: all in all, a sizeable force.

Although threat parameters increase the importance of in-place forces with a high degree of readiness, certain types of defensive operations will need to be left to reinforcing units. For example, the requirements for counter-air sorties and medium- and long-range interdiction to curb threats to vital installations and assets in BALTAP are clearly in excess of the capabilities of indigenous forces. Special missions like defence suppression, certain types of reconnaissance and airborne anti-armour warfare are also outside the scope of indigenous air forces.

In sheer numbers, the BALTAP area will need – and can accommodate – the influx of ten to fifteen squadrons of combat aircraft to secure sustainability and sufficient counter-offensive potential. Politically, the credibility of deterrence is dependent on the achievement of such parameters. On the ground, there is a need for at least one extra brigade-size manoeuvre unit on the island of Zealand and (probably more urgent) in Schleswig-Holstein–Jutland.

Reinforcements to BALTAP are therefore necessary in order to provide the defense of the Command with sufficient sustainability and efficient counter-offensive potential in face of the relevant threat. The present defense posture with regard to indigenous and reinforcements forces is based on the deterrent effect of collective defence and Allied commitment. This is especially important in an area which has no Allied forces stationed on a permanent basis. Reinforcements to BALTAP are vital politically as well as militarily. In the political sense, they are a clear and unambiguous signal to any potential aggressor of the will and ability of the Alliance to fulfil its commitments, if necessary *in extremis*. Possible reinforcements to BALTAP from Britain include the United Kingdom Mobile Force (UKMF), a number of squadrons of the Royal Air Force, and units of the UK/NL Marines. Of these forces, the two first mentioned components are, from a Danish point of view, of much more interest than the last. However, for the Island Commander, Faeroe Islands, Marine Forces are of primary importance to bolster the defence of the vital installations on these islands. These forces may also contribute a high-priority effort to defend oil and gas installations in the Danish part of the North Sea.

The UKMF and the Royal Air Force Squadrons can be deployed to BALTAP very quickly and smoothly, utilizing (Danish) civilian transport assets (and, to a lesser extent, certain Allied military lift assets). Prepositioning of ammunition, POL, and other consumables or material might improve transfer time scales and facilitate both the primary lift of the forces into BALTAP and their subsequent resupply. Further prepositioning must be considered one of the most cost-effective approaches to upgrade the combat value (as well as the sustainability) of (especially) the land element of the UKMF (1st Inf. BDE (UK) and logistic support units). Deployment of the UKMF and the Royal Air Force units to BALTAP take place on a regular basis, and detailed planning and co-operation with indigenous forces are developed to a very high degree of efficiency – a factor viewed with satisfaction by both parties.

1st Inf. BDE(UK) with its support units fits in very well in this context, not least due to the very positive time parameters, which are politically very valuable. A greater number of main battle tanks and some armoured personnel carriers would, however, provide the UKMF with much more flexibility and staying power, especially for possible operations in the Schleswig-Holstein area, where its present thin-skinned and rather immobile configuration may be less well suited. As this area may be its primary option in the future, this problem could taken on relevance in coming reviews of the force. The Royal Air Force Squadrons are a valuable addition to the fighter-bomber and close air-support assets in the area, and with USAF (and possibly USMC) units, they will almost meet the demand for air reinforcements.

Naturally, a Command as dependent on reinforcements as BALTAP must take steps to make sure that these reinforcements can be transported, deployed, and resupplied in the area of operations, and that they can fight in co-ordination and co-operation with indigenous forces. Logically, reinforcements should expect host nations to provide effective air defence during transfer and deployment (and area air defence under all circumstances), escort of forces at sea to the point of arrival, and rear area defence. Apart from these obligations, host nations provide a wide range of support, logistic, and medical services, parallel to those offered to indigenous forces.

In all of these fields, comprehensive improvements have taken place over the last few years, in Denmark as well as in Schleswig-Holstein. To point out only the most significant Danish efforts first, air defence has been drastically upgraded by the acquisition of several additional units of I-HAWK, adding depth to the belt area air defence of the northern part of BALTAP, and making it possible to concentrate air defence on vital points of arrival (like Esbjerg and the airfields of Jutland) or staging areas for indigenous or reinforcement units (in Jutland and in the islands) simultaneously. Short-range air defence in Schleswig-Holstein will be improved by the introduction of the next generation of shoulder-launched air defence missiles, which is due shortly. These measures will make the air defence assets of reinforcement forces available for the tasks for which they are intended: forward air defence of combat units, close-in defence of the logistic base, and additional air defence for key air stations. Area air defence of Danish air-space has also had the benefit of the introduction of the F-16 in its AD/FGA configuration, a factor which contributes greatly to the enhanced possibilities of establishing and preserving a permanently friendly air situation over BALTAP. On the German side, the introduction of Roland systems and other improvements in air defence have also contributed greatly to the overall improvement of air defence of BALTAP as a whole.

With respect to rear area defence, another concern of reinforcing units, the improvements are equally significant. On the German side, HEERES-MODEL 4 has introduced a great number of additional territorial units in Schleswig-Holstein, freeing the best-equipped territorial brigades and regiments to fill in as reserve forces behind the field units. In Denmark, the Jutland Combat Group will be upgraded, and modernizations will enhance the combat power of coastal combat groups. Furthermore, the Home Guard will be in a better shape to shoulder its manifold commitments, not least with respect to support to reinforcement units.

It should not be forgotten, either, that the Danish Frigate Squadron (for the first time in its NATO history) is able to offer escort capacity in Danish waters, and – to a limited degree – in the North Sea. This adds a most welcome augmentation to the NATO forces in these areas, and especially it provides air defence capabilities with a high degree of mobility.

BRITAIN AND THE SECURITY OF BALTAP: PARTNERSHIP NECESSARY

From a Danish – and a BALTAP – viewpoint, British participation in (and commitment to) the defence of the southernmost part of the North are essential, politically as well as militarily. Seen from Britain, these observations hold equally true. The security of the UK and the far North cannot be effectively defended without the contribution of BALTAP – its indigenous forces, provided by Denmark and Germany, and the extremely important facilities offered by geography as well as by man-made installations.

For all these reasons, the British reinforcements to BALTAP are perceived as a firm and unambiguous guarantee of Britain's commitment, and Danish authorites will to the utmost take advantage of the resources put at their disposal by the responsible politicians, to accommodate and support these reinforcements. The fact that Britain is situated close to BALTAP, and the fact that the British in general are regarded positively by an overwhelming majority of the Danish population (making reinforcements from Britain more palatable in Denmark than similar forces from, for example, the United States), increase the advantages in terms of transfer time and political adaptability. In the event of a crisis, the possible and foreseeable political consequences of calling in UK reinforcements might be thought to be especially beneficial. This would strengthen the likelihood of an early (and timely) request for reinforcements to BALTAP, and this in turn could maximize the deterrence factor, thereby increasing the chance of preventing crisis from developing into war.

Conference Discussion

Logistics are very important, though often squeezed out because they are at the bottom of most people's priority lists. This is a very weak area in the North European Command, although there is an evident determination on the part of SACEUR to do something about it in order to improve sustainability. Standards of training, morale and leadership also make an essential contribution to sustainability.

The scale of the support required is very considerable. Getting a squadron to Northern Norway requires 100 Hercules loads, half of which are filled with equipment which could be stockpiled in Norway, if only the Norwegians would agree. This would release the Hercules, which could go elsewhere (say BALTAP, where a further two squadrons will be sent). Given the size of the Hercules force all this would be a major task. Prestocking is particularly useful in the case of aircraft because we know where they are going to operate, which is not always the case for Army units.

Sometimes the British Forces suffer from what might be called the 'Western Desert' syndrome, namely the unconscious view that the place to which they are going is totally empty and has nothing to offer. In fact with their attitude to 'total defence', the Danes and the Norwegians have taken account of the availability of four-wheel drive vehicles, bulldozers and so on, to help reinforcing units. The British sometimes need to be reminded, for example, that when they go to Norway and Denmark, they do not need to take their own lager!

Another difficulty with sustainability is that being something of a bottomless bucket it can easily become very expensive, while at the same time not as glamorous as 'teeth' forces. Difficult decisions have to be made as to how long you want to sustain for; but as Admiral Watkins has recently pointed out investing in sustainability is a very effective (even cost-effective) deterrent. This is especially true against the Soviet Union given their apparent current aversion to the idea of a long war.

There is another problem with sustainability which is particularly true for forces like the Marines who prefer to fight light, but who need sustainability, which in turn leads to stocks which might slow them down. In their case prestocking is not the real answer because this would reduce their flexibility, as was the case for example when it was decided to preposition the stocks for a US Marine MAB in the

Trondelag area. Once they fly in and pick up their equipment they just become another land force, and not an amphibious one. In their case, though, they would take a very long time to arrive if they did *not* fly in, and so the Trondelag decision seems sensible – with other MABS possibly coming along later in an orthodox amphibious mode.

The fact that amphibious forces are essentially light keeps the sustainability and prestocking issue manageable. In Norway, an additional problem might be the fact that the UK/NL LF would be fighting Soviet Divisions which would be quite heavy. But when drawing the balance between firepower and mobility, the environment in which they have to operate needs to be taken into consideration as well. Even so, there are enhancements which the Marines would welcome, for example an increased area air defence capability and some improved artillery with more range and punch. To offset such deficiencies, of course, the Marines would try to take advantage of climate and terrain to exploit the difficulties that heavier (perhaps road-bound) forces would encounter in this area. Is it not their task to meet the main armoured thrust here or in BALTAP head on.

The great advantage that an amphibious force in fact offers the local Commander is its ability to lie off the coast, rather than be landed. The Marines' real value is in their capacity to be 'poised' off the enemy's front. Their special value would be lost if they were assigned to ordinary grinding, and attritional infantry operations ashore. The maximum unbalancing effect is achieved by keeping them not too heavily engaged so that they can be taken out if necessary. But to be able to move up and down freely they will need air security above them. For this there may well be an early need for offensive air operations against Soviet airfields in the Kola.

How vulnerable to air attack are the amphibious forces anyway? On the face of it, and with the experience of 1940 when command of the sea was more or less neutralized by command of the air, there would seem to be a serious danger of massed air-launched missile attack against large amphibious ships. The Falklands experience is not directly comparable because the geographic circumstances are different. In Norway there are mountains which rise 1000 metres straight from the side of a fjord. Large ships like LPDs would probably be much safer inside the fjords than they would stood off in the open sea from AS-4 air-launched missiles which are much more potent than Exocets.

Amphibious shipping can be put into fjords affording attacking aircraft only one avenue of approach, namely in from the sea where a good deal of anti-aircraft protection could be concentrated. Ships can also be kept on the move but there are practical problems with this kind of thing, especially in the communications area, and it may impede tactical flexibility especially with the smaller craft. With the clever reconnaissance technology available to the Soviet Union, it would not be easy to hide completely, even so; but certainly the fjords would help very considerably.

Once the amphibious forces are landed their support ships can be readily dispersed around the fjords, provided they can be protected from naval threats as well. They can certainly be hidden better than land support forces which have to be concentrated on or near a single road. The UK/NL AF and the United States MAB brigades are about the same size as the Norwegian regiments that would be going up to reinforce the North, but are better placed in being able to disperse and conceal their logistic backing. As US Navy Secretary Lehman has recently observed, ships which can move are bound to be less vulnerable than large stockpiles which cannot. Keeping these resources afloat is a great operational advantage also in that the forces can readily be re-embarked and moved somewhere else, if conditions ashore require it.

The Soviet Naval Infantry in this area, which effectively amounts to one brigade, is a force for local rather than strategic operations. We can more or less discount the prospect of their being used in a direct assault on the Tromso area, but the Soviet helicopter-borne force is increasing and does cause concern. CINCNORTH's greatest worry is the prospect of a Soviet thrust through Schleswig-Holstein. While it is true that the German and Danish navies properly supported by air have a very reasonable chance of defending Zealand and the Danish islands, the Soviet overland threat must be taken very seriously. Despite the very strong German division and the Danish reinforcements coming down from the north to help defend the area, the Soviet Union might well be able to break through here. Having done so, they could turn north, staying within the Northern Europe Command (NEC) or (more worryingly still) turn south, threatening the Central Front itself.

Although the advantages of flexibility are acknowledged, the Danes would like some Allied forces committed to their defence. It is very difficult to make plans in situations where the arrival of some of the key players cannot be assumed. How, for example would the UK/NL AF operate in Danish waters? Given the present consensus that now it is no longer possible simply to land the forces and then take the shipping away, letting the troops ashore to get on with it, it would certainly be more difficult for amphibious forces to operate here than in Norway, because of the air situation and the absence of fjords. Nonetheless this continues to be a viable deployment option, and there is a well-protected base not far away in Southern Norway.

The UKMF is the only dedicated land reinforcement for BALTAP, providing the third manoeuvre element in Schleswig-Holstein. The continuance of this land commitment is therefore very important to the Danes for political as well as military reasons. Denmark would welcome more prepositioning and stockpiling; Danes and Germans must not be left to defend this vital area alone. Although the Royal Marines would be welcome, too, the military justification for sending them to Schleswig-Holstein is much less; this is not their kind of operation. Cutting the UKMF on the other hand would create a dangerous hole through the Northern Flank in one of its most important and most vulnerable areas.

In connection with this area, finally, it is often suggested that the command boundaries in Northern Europe are wrong, and of course no boundaries are ever quite right. The southern boundary of CINCNORTH on the Elbe is arguable. Should there be a land boundary running down a river? There is also a case for North Norway being looked after by those who look after the Norwegian Sea, though Scandinavians would not like to see their area being divided between NATO commands. Perhaps there is a case for moving the NEC boundary out to sea a little from the present 12-mile line. Complicated as they are, existing boundaries in that area are probably just about right.

Part VI
Options and Conclusions

15 Future Policy Options
Admiral Sir James Eberle, GCB

Throughout more than 30 years, concern has been expressed over the security of NATO's Northern Flank. This concern is normally related to the adequacy of the allocated force levels, and to the speed at which the designated external reinforcement forces can be brought in. The vital importance of the Baltic Approaches to the defence of NATO's Central Region, and of the Norwegian Sea to the security of the Atlantic sea lanes, make the Northern Flank posture both in political and military terms an integral part of the Alliance's overall security. However, the remoteness of its northernmost reaches from major Western military bases, its very close proximity to the major Soviet bases in the Kola Peninsula, the difficult problems that its climate and terrain present for air, sea and ground operations, and the political environment of the Nordic area, all combine to provide unique limitations to its effective defence.

WHAT IS NEW?

In the face of the increasing strength of Soviet forces, and particularly the growth of the Soviet Northern Fleet, gradual improvements have been made in the Allied position. These have inevitably cost money. With the defence budgets of all countries coming under heavy pressure, there are likely to be increasing difficulties in maintaining this pattern of improvement; and it may indeed not be possible, without a change in priorities, to retain in full the existing capabilities. The British defence budget after seven years of expansion at an annual rate of growth of about 3 per cent is now facing a period of at least three years of expenditure reducing at not less than 2 per cent per annum. In Norway, it has been estimated that the reduction in the price of oil and the weakening of the US dollar may reduce the government's tax revenue by an amount significantly greater than the total defence budget for 1986. In the US, the Gramm–Rudman amendment could have major implications for defence spending. In Britain, this problem of budget pressure has already manifested itself in the decision of whether (and how), to maintain the amphibious lift capability for the UK/NL LF available for the defence of Northern Norway. Before examining what alternative policy options might be available for Britain and which might result in effective security for the Northern Flank at a lower level of cost, it is sensible to consider what else is new.

In addition to budget pressure, defence policy decision-making must be seen against a background of changing public attitudes in Europe towards security. Whilst there remains throughout Western Europe widespread concern about the role of nuclear weapons in Alliance strategy, and about the number and character of the nuclear weapon arsenals of the two Superpowers, there is also a widespread belief that nuclear deterrence does work; and that there is not likely to be a war in Europe in the near (or even medium-term) future. Put another way, there is an increasing belief that 'what is enough to deter' need not go on growing – and, indeed, may perhaps be able to be reduced. This belief is motivated as much by the absence of a direct feeling of threat from Moscow, as it is by the changing priorities for government expenditure. Maintaining defence expenditure is no longer a 'vote winner' in Europe. In Britain the Labour Party has committed itself to a policy of 'non-nuclear defence', a policy that seems unlikely to be changed even if the Party were to come to power at the next Election. With this policy comes the implied commitment to strengthen conventional defence. Whilst there can be no guarantee that money saved by the abandonment of British nuclear weapons would in practice be made available for defence spending, there would be strong pressure upon a Labour government to make some increase in spending on conventional weapons as the price for giving up a nuclear capability. This could provide an opportunity for reviewing British defence priorities.

The lack of immediacy in the threat perceived in Western Europe from Moscow has its origins in a number of factors. One is the apparently increasing willingness of the US administration to use force – as in the anti-terrorist bombing of Tripoli. As the US appears more militant, so the Soviet Union appears (in relative terms) to be less threatening. A second factor is the success of Soviet propaganda in presenting a picture of the Soviet Union as a nation which is sincerely pursuing paths towards a peaceful settlement of the East–West dispute. Finally there is a slowly growing belief that in Eastern Europe and the Soviet Union there has started a process of long-term change, whose eventual result may be a breaking down of the present

European divide, and the creation of a new European security system which is not seen as a threat by either side.

As part of this perception of long-term and gradual change in the European security system, there is increasing recognition that the continuation of the present levels of US force levels in Europe cannot be guaranteed. However, West European governments are anxious that the present US commitment should not be undermined by the perception that Europe is not doing enough in its own defence. Europe is, therefore, making considerable efforts to strengthen the European pillar of the Atlantic Alliance and to 'get its act together', even though these efforts result in seemingly very slow progress. However, even where the US has indicated signs of strong commitment to Europe – as in the new US Maritime Strategy of forward defence at sea – there are as many in Europe who are concerned at its implications as there are those who welcome it.

A particular problem of this strategy in relation to the Northern Flank is seen to be its emphasis on early forward deployment and on warfighting, despite similar emphasis on its global, defensive and deterrent nature. In his article published in the January 1986 edition of the Proceedings of the US Naval Institute, the Chief of Naval Operations, Admiral Jim Watkins makes the specific point that the forward deployment of carrier battle groups in the Norwegian Sea 'does not imply some immediate "charge of the Light Brigade" on the Kola Peninsula'. Nevertheless, the strategy has been widely seen as emphasizing the USN's readiness to conduct conventional war at sea; and it is this perception that provides a focus for fundamental tension between the interests of the two sides of the Atlantic. Because the US would bear the first and principal costs of nuclear war, there is a strong interest on the part of the US in wishing to raise the 'nuclear threshold' so as to reduce to a minimum the chance that a nuclear war would ever be fought. In Europe, however, there is just as great an interest in ensuring that a war with conventional weapons is never again fought; and thus there is concern lest the 'nuclear threshold' be raised so high by the US that the chance of a 'conventional' war is enhanced.

A final factor of change that we need to consider is in the field of new weaponry. The sea-launched cruise missile, in its nuclear and conventionally-headed land attack versions, represents a new means of threatening attack on the Soviet Navy's Northern bases and of carrying out airfield interdiction and denial strikes. Previously such attacks could be mounted only at short range from the Norwegian airfields in North Norway, or at long range from bases outside the area, or from carrier-borne strike aircraft from carriers operating in the Norwegian Sea. Each of these operations involved a high degree of risk. Now, such attacks can be launched from the comparative safety of submerged submarines or from smaller surface warships. This capability could have important implications for the operational viability and thus the effectiveness and importance of both the Soviet and Norwegian Northern airfields.

SOME CHALLENGES

The Nato strategy of 'deterrence' is based on a policy of 'defence and *détente*'. Unfortunately the requirements of deterrence and defence have become increasingly confused in the search for *détente*. The important relationship between deterrence and defence concerns the need for credibility; for it is the credibility that (if deterrence should fail) the defence might be successful that makes the deterrence effective. However, the requirements (either in political or military terms) of deterrence and defence are not necessarily coincident. For deterrent purposes, it may well be important to demonstrate a particular reinforcement capability. Should deterrence fail, it is not necessary to employ that reinforcement capability in the way that has been demonstrated. It may be desirable as part of a policy of deterrence to operate Allied surface warships well North in the Norwegian Sea; should deterrence fail and war break out, it would probably not make sense (in view of Soviet submarine and naval air strength in the area) to try to operate them in that region.

Not only do we need to keep such differences clearly in mind; we also need to be aware of the danger of believing that, because we can demonstrate a particular military capability in peace, that capability is necessarily a feasible operation in war. The 'fog and uncertainty' of war makes even the simple things difficult, and it is not an abstract quality. It is a quality that pervades every phase of operations. When a man knows that a principal task of his opponent is to kill him, it concentrates the mind on aspects of war that can never wholly be reproduced in exercises or peacetime practice. It is important therefore that we learn to avoid military 'party tricks'.

The Northern Command of Allied Command Europe (ACE) is usually described as a single entity and its defence requirements are seen to be indivisible. This is understandable – and, in some perspectives, correct. But it is also misleading. The three regions of

North Norway, South Norway and the Baltic Approaches each need separate consideration. The defence of Denmark and BALTAP is vital to the defence of the left flank of NATO's ground and air position in Central Europe. The principal threat to it lies from a Soviet ground attack through Schleswig-Holstein. It is also vulnerable to air and amphibious attack across the Baltic. A battle on the Central Front without involving the BALTAP area is thus impossible. It is also less vulnerable to direct attack, unless the Soviets are prepared to accept the risks involved in the violation of Swedish neutrality.

However the Northern Flank is considerably more than the Northern Command of ACE, for it includes the sea area extending to (and under) the ice to the north, and in the east to the GIUK Gap. This sea area plays a very important role both in the security and defence of Norway and in the defence of the Atlantic Sea Lines of Communication (SLOCs), with Iceland holding a key pivotal position. Within this area there are also a number of other islands (such as the Faeroe and Shetland groups) which, whilst not having the strategic importance of Iceland would nevertheless be of very high value to the Soviets if they were to fall under their control in war. There is also the island of Svalbard, the territory of which is of Norwegian ownership but with an international regime. Its strategic value in war is doubtful, but it is important as a potential source of Soviet–NATO pressure and conflict. These islands are too often forgotten in our planning.

Whilst the linkages between the defence of the Central Front and the Baltic Approaches, between the Baltic Approaches and South Norway, between South Norway and North Norway and between the Norwegian Sea and North Norway are self-evident and almost universally accepted, the reciprocal linkage between the defence of the Norwegian Sea and the security of Northern Norway is more open to challenge. The vital question is whether (if the Soviets were to seize and hold North Norway) this would inevitably result in the Norwegian Sea becoming an area of Soviet sea control. Put in a different way, would the failure of forward defence on land in North Norway also lead to the failure of forward defence at sea? The key to answering this question rests in an assessment of the role of the North Norwegian airfields. With the exception of Andoya, which operates long-range maritime patrol (LRMP) aircraft, these airfields chiefly operate Fighter Ground Attack (FGA) aircraft. In the event of a Soviet attack on North Norway, whilst the air defence cover that these latter aircraft would indirectly provide for inshore naval operations would be valuable, it is difficult to see these limited fighter resources being continuously available offshore for the tactical air support of maritime operations (TASMO). Nor are the ground attack capabilities of these aircraft suited to the attack of Soviet ships at sea. However, the loss of Andoya (and thus the maritime air reconnaissance, anti-submarine and anti-surface capability of its LRMP aircraft), together with the possible loss of other tactical maritime facilities in the Northern area, would undoubtedly result in a significant reduction of Allied maritime capability in the North Norwegian Sea. But it is far from clear that this factor would prove decisive in the battle for sea control (particularly for submarine operations) and in preventing the Soviets from reaching a new 'start line' at the GIUK Gap for their surface and submarine operations in the Atlantic.

What would, however, be far more serious would be if the Soviets were to capture these airfields and then be able to mount their own intensive air operations from them. This would be no easy task for the Soviets since it can reasonably be expected that last-minute demolition of the runways and of the other vital airfield facilities would have been carried out by the Norwegians. The airfields would also be under threat from interdiction by Allied air attacks and by sea launched cruise missiles. The conduct of air operations in war with sophisticated modern aircraft – as opposed to their operation in peacetime exercise flying – is a very complex task requiring a high degree of logistic back-up, even under the most favourable conditions. Under adverse conditions, it becomes an extremely suspect operation of war. Provided, therefore, that the Soviets are not permitted the 'free' use of these North Norwegian airfields, and provided that NATO shore-based long-range fighter aircraft flying from the UK and Iceland can be used to offer a threat to prevent the extension too far south of Soviet LRMP operations, there is no reason for the allies to assume the loss of sea control throughout the Norwegian Sea.

BRITAIN'S INTERESTS

In seeking new policy options for Britain in the defence of NATO's Northern Flank, it is necessary first to be clear as to Britain's interests. The first of these must be the political solidarity and military effectiveness of the NATO Alliance. Without political cohesion amongst the Atlantic nations the effectiveness of deterrence is put at risk. Without the collective military capabilities of all the Allied nations being used in concert, then the military strength of the allies may not be sufficient for the defence strategy of flexibility in response to be effective. There are, at present, very considerable strains and stresses in the trans-Atlantic relationship. Some will say that it has ever been thus, and that there is no cause for alarm. Others argue that there are now new trends which are eroding some of the factors which underlie the fundamental stability of the European–American relationship. In either case, there is a need for renewed awareness on both sides of the Atlantic of the dangers of disunity.

Britain's own relations with Norway need to be seen in the context of the North Sea as well as the Atlantic. The two countries are North Sea littoral powers. They have a long-standing and close cultural and trading relationship. They straddle the important oil and gas fields of the Northern North Sea. As the United States and Western Europe need each other, so do Britain and Norway. But Norway's position is (in both a geographic and a political sense) somewhat set apart from that of the other countries of Western Europe. Norway is not a member of the EC, and does not take part in the processes of European political co-operation, which are beginning to have undertones in the field of European security. Norway is not a member of the WEU, an organization that is now trying to revitalize itself and to find an appropriate role within the future structure of West European security. This results in a certain sense of isolation in Norway. Britain, of all the European nations, has a special responsibility and interest in ensuring that this sense of isolation does not result in the Norwegian people becoming disillusioned with the concept of collective security within the wider European framework.

A further factor which has heightened Norwegian discomfort at living so close to the 'Russian bear' has been the influence of the Soviet Northern Fleet. Its increasing size and power, and the extensive bases which support it, give to the Soviet Union a large and growing interest in Northern waters. As the size of the Northern Fleet has grown, so has its confidence and competence. As a natural consequence, Soviet naval operations have spread south towards the GIUK Gap and the Atlantic. These are, of course, the 'high seas' and the Soviet Navy has as much of a legitimate right to operate in these waters as has any other Navy. But so do other navies have a legitimate right to operate in the international waters of the far North. It is an important British, Norwegian and NATO interest that the Soviets are not permitted to regard any of these seas as a *mare sovieticum*.

Iceland is a member of NATO but does not supply any military forces. It does, however, provide facilities for the air base at Keflavik.

The Soviet Navy has a very long passage from its Northern Fleet bases to a position in which its submarines, surface ships or aircraft can effectively threaten Allied reinforcement and resupply from the United States to Europe. Defence in depth, starting from as far north and east as possible, is clearly the most effective concept of NATO operations to counter the threat to the Atlantic SLOCs. But additionally, the 'choke point' provided by the GIUK Gap provides the opportunity for NATO forces to choose a 'battleground' which is to their best advantage for surveillance in peace and for fighting in war. To be able to exploit this battleground requires that Iceland and its facilities for operating LRMP and fighter aircraft are available to the allies. The defence of Iceland (together with the territorial defence of the Faeroe and Shetland Islands – the latter containing a major British terminal for the extraction of North Sea oil) are specific and particular British interests.

Finally, there is a clear British interest in the prevention of crisis on the Northern Flank. Much has been written on the subject of 'crisis control' in NATO, and much has been achieved. Nevertheless, there is still much work to be done, both in theory and practice (and particularly in such difficult areas as de-escalation) before NATO could fairly claim to be satisfied that it has a fully effective crisis control organization. Relatively little attention has, however, been given to 'crisis avoidance' – the problem of how to prevent crises arising, rather than controlling them after they have begun. A major factor in crisis avoidance is the recognition of those areas which are a potential source of friction, and thus of possible crisis. One such area is Svalbard. It is therefore a matter of concern that so little attention seems to be paid to it either by the British or NATO authorities. Svalbard could easily become the 'Berlin' of the Northern Flank.

WHAT ARE THE OPTIONS?

In seeking alternative policy options, it needs to be recognized that radical change presents enormous political difficulties and is most unlikely to be conducive to Allied cohesion, whilst practicable change is likely to be possible only in small incremental steps. In real life, we do not start with a clean sheet of paper and we are in practice bound by political and military realities. The first policy option is to do nothing. For, unless there is good reason for change, there is good reason for no change. This is an easy option, and is therefore one which has wide appeal; unfortunately, it is not likely to be available, for the reasons (principally of defence budget pressures) that have been discussed above. A second option is to accept that external reinforcement by sea or air of North Norway is not a practicable operation of war – only of deterrence. The effect of this would be that the UK/NL AF would be regarded and equipped not as a reinforcement force but as pre-enforcement force – that is, one that is designed to get there before fighting has broken out, not after. This would not remove the need for the force's specialized amphibious shipping for its commando helicopter lift. But it could reduce the complexity of much of its presently required operational capability. A natural corollary of such a policy of pre-enforcement (linked to the concept that NATO's principal military interest in this region is to deny to the Soviet's the use of the North Norwegian airfields, rather than to retain them for Allied use) would be to move towards a policy on (and of early resort to) guerrilla tactics. Of course, it would not be sensible to abandon ground unless faced with greatly superior force; as it would also not be sensible to retain maritime support forces in the area in the face of an air threat that could in the near term lead only to the loss of those ships. But the very early planned use of guerrilla warfare, aimed principally at denying effective use of North Norway's to Soviet forces, could yield significant savings.

A third option would be to adopt a policy of prepositioning the equipment of the UK/NL AF in Norway. In this case, specialized amphibious shipping would not be essential. The option would, however, lead to severe limitations for the operational deployment of the force, and in the flexibility of its use. It would also present political problems for the Norwegian government, although the acceptance of the policy of prepositioning for the equipment for one US MAB provides a precedent. Such prepositioning would provide a sensible financial option for the UK only if the government decided that it had no other external commitments that required the retention of specialized amphibious shipping.

A policy option for the Royal Navy would be to make a shift of maritime priorities away from the task of contributing to the direct defense (principally ASW) of the Atlantic SLOCs towards the task of 'containing' the Soviet Navy in the waters of the North Norwegian Sea. It is not immediately clear what the extent of the implications for naval force structure would be. It could be considerable, since the characteristics of this relatively closed area of sea contrast greatly with those pertaining to the expanses of the Atlantic Ocean. Only a detailed examination could establish whether significant savings might be obtained without unacceptable penalties in other areas. There is also a clear case of examining the implications of increasing the priority for UK Home defense towards the Northern boundaries of the United Kingdom, and for a shift of emphasis for naval deployments and exercises towards the north. A policy option for the British Army would be to reconsider the reinforcement role of the UKMF.

Whatever options are considered, however, fundamental decisions can sensibly be taken only in the light of a judgement as to the relative priority to be given to the role of British forces in contributing to the security of the Northern Flank when compared with the Central Front. At present (at least within the informal agreement of the UK Chiefs of Staff) they apparently rate an equal priority. But it seems unlikely that the Chiefs of Staff will be able to indulge in this luxury of non-decision for very much longer. When the time for choice does arrive, it may well be that the military factors, and Britain's interests as an island nation, dictate that first priority should go to the Northern Flank and to maritime capabilities. However, Britain's wider interests in the building of a newly united Europe, and the political difficulties which would attend an attempt to make reductions in the capability of Britain's ground and air forces in Central Europe, or that would weaken NATO's capability for forward defence in Germany, are such that it seems likely that political pragmatism may well again triumph over military logic.

Conference Discussion

Discussion turned on the geographical extent of the Northern Flank. Naturally, the tendency was to concentrate on the familiar areas of Northern Norway and the Baltic Approaches, but there are other important areas, too, which do not get so much coverage. Iceland, for all its obvious strategic importance, is often forgotten in such discussions. In fact the Icelanders show (by such subtle signs as the seting up of a Defence Section in their Ministry of Foreign Affairs) a growing awareness of the implications for them of recent strategic developments. It may not be entirely fanciful to see something of the same thing in neutral Ireland, for all the narrowness of its defence traditions.

Greenland and the Faeroes are important, too, not least in that some of the installations there greatly help Britain's air defence. It is worth making the point that Denmark makes large annual subsidies to both, and that these subsidies ought really to be regarded as part of her defence effort. A lot of this money goes into improving the infrastructure of what is in effect the Left Flank for the Commander of NATO's Strike Fleet, Atlantic. The Danes are building several airfields up along the coast which will be capable of taking aircraft of the size of the Hercules, and Greenland's existing airfields are open for 320 days a year on average. Although the Danes are obviously not going to militarize the place, the work they are doing could have military value in ten–fifteen years' time. It might even attract Soviet interest. Although it is hard to see at the moment how the Soviet Union could threaten them, such a possibility cannot altogether be disregarded.

Svalbard is another important but often neglected part of the Northern Flank. Annoyed by the fact that it is Norwegian, the Soviet Union tried after the Second World War to turn Svalbard into a bilateral condominium. Under the Paris Treaty, the powers agreed that it should not be used for warlike purposes, but it obviously has strategic significance. The climate and geographical conditions up there would allow regular military operations most of the time. Svalbard after all does have a modern airstrip, with a proper surface, 2000 m long. It takes 125 flights a year, with only fourteen cancellations over the past ten years. The airstrip is usually operational for all but ten days a year, and it would be perfectly feasible to operate a fighter squadron up there. What would NATO do with its Nimrods if there were Foxbats on Svalbard?

The Soviet Union has also won for itself a strong commercial presence on the island. It has about 2000 people up there, compared to the 1000 Norwegians, and their main reason for being there is coal-mining; the Norwegians nevertheless extract about 50 per cent more coal that the Russians. The Soviet Union has connected disputes with Norway over fisheries and sea boundaries. Britain does not always support Norway as it might, possibly putting short-term commercial interests before long-term strategic ones.

It is hard to deny that the Northern Flank has much more prominence now than it once had. In Germany, for example, interest in the Northern Flank has grown considerably over the past few years. A bigger American presence in the Indian Ocean, and the growing American interest in the countries of the Pacific Rim have reduced US naval force levels in the Atlantic. In turn this means that the Norwegian European navies might have to assume a greater prominence in making the first responses in a crisis on the Northern Flank. For this reason, Germany in 1980 lifted nationally-imposed restrictions which had hitherto limited German naval operations to the Dover–Calais line and 61° North. This would allow NATO to use German naval forces more flexibly. Despite its position on the Central Front, Germany is a Northern Flank nation, too.

The Dutch also take the Northern Flank seriously. Many politicians regard it as a useful area for the prevention (or at least containment) of East–West crisis. Nevertheless 70 per cent of the Dutch defence effort is devoted to the Central Front, for very obvious geographic reasons. About 20 per cent goes on ASW and the protection of NATO's SLOCs. The Netherlands has built an ASW fleet of eighteen frigates with another four to come, so this particular response to the growing Soviet naval threat is well supported. Although there is a growing sense that the Northern Flank is important, and although there is every intention of continuing to participate in the UK/NL LF, an expansion of the Dutch role in the North (possibly at the expense of the Navy's ASW role) would at best be incremental. And every step would require significant shifts of opinion amongst the military, as well as the politicians.

Denmark, being in the Northern Flank area, has little problem in accepting its importance, but outsiders do frequently comment adversely on Denmark's attitude to the NATO Alliance as a whole. In fact, regular opinion polls show that only between 10–15 per cent of the population are against NATO, with 60–70 per cent being in favour. In practice, neutralist ideas in Denmark are dead. Even Denmark's Socialist and Social Democratic parties are taking a notably softer line on NATO. Anti-Americanism is no more strongly rooted in Denmark than it is in Germany (and, where it exists, tends to focus only on some aspects of current American policy, and not on American values). Should the 1987 Elections produce a Social Democratic government, there is little prospect of more than minor changes.

All this may make possible the kind of multi-national approach on the Northern Flank which many would see as an important element both of deterrence and of crisis prevention. What about NATO having a standing force in the area? While it would not be easy to produce the necessary units, it might nonetheless be a good idea. The idea apparently originated with the Dutch but was eventually discarded because it ran the risk of undermining STANAFORLANT. Maybe the answer would be to deploy STANAVFORLANT much further north? There is also a good deal to be said for improving operational co-operation at the planning level. In this connection, Germany has been active in updating NATO's Concept of Maritime Operations (CONMAROPS), and has urged further development and further harmonization so that the best collective use is made of available assets. It is clearly better not to leave this kind of consideration of 'what to do when' to the last minute, when the pressure is on. The time to do planning is when you have the time to sit around and bring in academic and other specialists. At the highest level, NATO has the strategy of Flexible Response, and the maritime connotations of this have to be worked out rigorously. It is vital that NATO works out a series of possible plans; while NATO should not be hypnotized by its own planning, the more plans it has the more flexible it can be. Perhaps the US Navy's Maritime Strategy has rather pre-empted NATO on this?

Finally, there would seem to be some justification for having an unclassified version of the CONMAROPS which could be talked about by NATO spokesmen, if only to counter widespread impressions that the Maritime Strategy was concocted in Washington by political people for political purposes. The two are, after all, very much along the same lines.

Concluding Remarks
Lawrence Freedman

The discussions in this volume have confronted the difficulty of defining the Northern Flank as a distinct region in strategic terms. Much of its strategic significance derives from its likely role in events that might be set in motion elsewhere in the world. In the weeks leading up to the 1986 conference there were two clear reminders of the interdependence that demonstrates the difficulty of viewing any region in isolation. In April 1986, an attack was ordered from Washington involving aircraft from bases in Britain as well as from carriers in the Mediterranean against targets in Tripoli. This demonstrated the reach of modern military power. In May, an accident at a nuclear reactor in the Soviet Union led to fallout spreading throughout Europe. The Soviet Union through its own incompetence managed to harm adversaries, allies and neutrals alike. Such a radiation cloud – the most chilling symbol of the modern age – is insidious; it mocks national boundaries and spheres of influence, as well as declarations of neutrality and nuclear freedom.

The task of strategic studies is to try to understand the sort of interconnections highlighted by these events, and to draw out their implications. Nonetheless, there is also a risk of taking the proposition that 'everything is connected with everything else' too far. If a problem is phrased in excessively broad terms it becomes unmanageable. Moreover, while the compartments may be artificial, they gain reality from the probability that strategic actors will in practice think and act in compartmentalized terms. The important links drawn out by the analyses in this volume may not actually be revealed in practice, simply because those involved do not follow this logic so rigorously. There is therefore still some point in considering the North as a distinctive region in itself, however much this volume quite properly emphasizes its interrelationship with other regions.

We have been considering a series of countries which have thought long and hard over many years about their security problems, coming to terms both with their geography and their past experience. The North's security problems are not based on any sense that the North itself is politically unstable. We are not thinking of a Norwegian–Swedish war (at least for the moment), in the same way that we cannot ignore the possibility of a Greek–Turkish conflict on NATO's Southern Flank. This is not an area of chronic political upheaval. Clive Archer (Chapter 1) described some new stresses and strains, but nobody would suggest that the situation is explosive, and that makes it qualitatively different from any other stretch of the periphery of the Soviet Union where political instability tends to be endemic. It is often said that the Soviet Union's main security problem is that it is surrounded by hostile Communist states. This is one of the parts of the world where it is not. Elsewhere, it has to think about the civil war in Afghanistan, the unsettled satellites of Eastern Europe, the disputed Sino–Soviet border. In Northern Europe there is no hostile Communist state: only sensitive capitalist states which have worked out their own forms of accommodation to Soviet power, seeking to deter without provoking.

In all these circumstances, the countries of this region ought to be left to look after themselves, drawing on their substantial political and diplomatic strengths as much as their inevitably limited military strength. It is their fate that this is not possible. It is a fate that they became only too aware of during the Second World War. This is an experience that none want to repeat. Their basic security problem is that by virtue of geography they are in the way of attempts by other variations to solve their own. Johan Jørgen Holst (Chapter 3) suggests that it is the responsibility of those from both East and West who wish to sort out their security problems in the Nordic area to respect the fact that this is in some way an intrusion. Their pressure is the product of particular geographic and political conditions; they must be sensitive to local feelings. The inability of the Soviet Union to show such respect and sensitivity is one of the major reasons why NATO's position is far less dire in this part of the world than one might otherwise have reason to expect. By pushing what Malcolm Mackintosh (Chapter 4) translated as a notion of a 'maritime frontier' ever southwards, the Soviet Union has made the countries of this area very much aware of the extent to which it would have no hesitation in sorting out *its* security problems in whatever way it felt appropriate. It is no comfort to be told that the Soviet Union is pursuing a defensive strategy when one finds oneself on the wrong side of this defensive frontier. All this requires that NATO makes clear that the Soviet Union must never presume that these are their seas in which its rights must always take precedence. This message is important not only for reasons of deterrence, but because in practice NATO could not allow the Soviet Union to have such presumptions in war. It is far better that these matters be understood well beforehand rather than suddenly and crudely asserted at the last moment. Jeremy Moore (Chapter 11) reminded us in connection with the Falklands that it would have done everybody a lot of good if there had been a greater clarity about what importance the UK in fact attached to the Falklands, or at least if it had disabused Buenos Aires about the assumptions made as to the likely response to a seizure of the islands. These are not easy messages to convey in the midst of a crisis.

It became clear in the conference that these requirements have become much more important, and much more difficult. This is in part because of the role of these seas in Soviet SSBN operations. Given trends in the strategic balance, there is no reason to believe that this role will become anything other than more important in the future, in part because of a fear of a future 'battle of the Atlantic', with vigorous Soviet movement through the GIUK Gap against NATO's SLOCs, and because of the opportunities for an outflanking movement via the North directed towards the Centre. It was brought home by the First Sea Lord (Chapter 5) and also by Jonathan Alford (Chapter 6) that from the British point of view this is an area which is really rather uncomfortably close. Britain tends as a nation to look southwards, Britons go south for their holidays, Britons go south to locate industry, and have usually gone south to fight wars. It does no harm (and I speak with feeling as a northerner) occasionally to look north, to what is coming up on what is considered in the British mental set to be the 'rear'. As Jonathan Alford made clear, this shift has already begun and is reflected in the greater concern with air defences. The question at the heart of this conference was whether more should be done to reflect this sensation of threat that was in no way so strong even a decade ago.

Before discussing whether NATO can actually organize such a shift in priorities, let us consider what sort of shift it should be. I am not competent to comment on what I found to be fascinating discussions concerning the particular tactical problems and requirements of NATO forces in this area (Chapters 7–15). Some broad themes that were raised are worth addressing, especially the question of the 'Forward Strategy' of the United States. I have been reassured that this strategy is not that new, but then there is very little in Alliance terms that can be *that* new after 40 years. But even shifts in emphasis can have major repercussions in such a long-standing Alliance, because this has become a delicate collection of mutual understandings, concerns and sensitivities that it is best not to upset. Sometimes NATO will overstress this delicacy, and overstate the problems of change. NATO then becomes an Alliance driven by inertia: because something has always been done that way, that this must be the way for the future. Nevertheless those proposing shifts in emphasis must recognize that even marginal changes have repercussions.

From the discussions in this volume there is clearly no lack of support for the proposition that the American Navy should operate actively in the Norwegian Sea. The main concern may be with the rhetoric that surrounds this activity. In a peacetime Alliance, rhetoric is not a 'free good', not just something to be used in one context with the assumption that it can be played down and pushed to the side in another. Robust statements of military intent which find a ready and appreciative audience in Washington can appear as downright provocative in the area of their proposed application. One concern with the Forward Strategy relates to the trailing of Soviet SSBNs. It may be helpful that the Soviet Union is concerned about the vulnerability of its SSBNs and devotes as much resources as possible to their protection, but the issue of how far the US would pursue these SSBNs in practice in a crisis, or more seriously in war, is an important one. Could NATO afford to be too successful at this task? Would NATO dare to attrit the Soviet SSBN force to the point where it actually looked as though it was wasting so fast that unless something was done quickly the Soviet Union would find itself vulnerable to the loss of its retaliatory capability? This sort of 'use it or lose it' issue is already recognized on the Central Front as a potential source of nuclear instability. The line between putting the other side on its guard and actually pushing it into a corner could become very fine indeed.

Another and related issue concerns the extent to which NATO has actually thought through the risks of a maritime confrontation in this area which had been prompted by little else but the degree of activity under way in a crisis. NATO may be moving through the GIUK Gap hurriedly enforcing its position in the northern Norwegian Sea, while the Warsaw Pact Fleet might be moving out of the Gap (or at least towards it to meet this threat), and possibly (and more ambitiously) to interfere with Western shipping. Is there not a risk of an awkward clash arising simply out of a concern not to be put at too much of a disadvantage at such a time (remembering that while a crisis is being managed few can be sure for certain that it will, in the end, be managed). This could produce a catastrophic result that neither side wanted or expected. If we are trailing and harrying, if we are mobilizing and maneuvring, then at the very least the rules of engagement are going to be extremely important. This argues for reviving the US–Soviet talks that have addressed this sort of question in the past.

Another risk with the 'Forward Strategy' is what one might call 'Duke of York-ism', where you lead people up to the top of the hill and then have to lead them down again. There is a risk of pronouncing as a real policy a set of desiderata and then proclaiming it obtained when in fact you have not quite made it, and may even have to go into reverse. There are two risks: one is a simple letdown so that claims in the future would lose credibility; another is that the Soviet Union may still respond. This may be what happened with the Alliance in the 1960s with 'flexible response'. Unfortunately it was the Soviet Union which took flexible response most seriously with regards to its conventional forces. Meanwhile, Western Europe insisted that one of the conditions for accepting flexible response was that it should involve minimal extra costs. A result of the promotion of the new doctrine was thus a worsening of NATO's conventional position because the Warsaw Pact in the end took it more seriously than did NATO. The question of the sustainability of the 'forward strategy' is therefore critical. Can we carry through such a policy, particularly in these days of budgetary stringency, unless it is based on a firm consensus and not just the latest bright ideas to emerge from Washington?

A final problem is the question of the relationship between deterrence and warfighting. There is a distinction between the two. This can suffer if the deterrers take it too far and argue that in deterring the Soviet Union capabilities and doctrine are almost irrelevant so long as the Soviet Union has reason to think that NATO *might* do something if provoked. It has been a natural shift in strategic thinking over the last decade to insist on the reintegration of the operational element into deterrence. However, what deters is not only the quality of NATO fighting forces but also the quality of the Alliance. It does NATO no good at all if in the effort to push through a shift in strategy the whole Alliance structure is weakened as a result. In the end, the Alliance is in itself the most formidable thing that the Soviet Union has to confront. This is a very irritating view to those who look at things in a purely operational sense, but it has to be accommodated. The challenge is not to despair but to explore those things that can be Alliance-reinforcing while also militarily valuable. Sir James Eberle (Chapter 15) indicated how this approach could develop. The need is for measures which improve matters operationally without being too provocative or risk setting in motion an interaction between the two opposing sides that could rapidly get out of hand and deny diplomacy the opportunity to come up with a peaceful settlement.

There is a particular twist to this problem in the area that Jeremy Moore discussed (Chapter 11): logistics and sustainability. It would be nice to believe that sustainability improves deterrence; unfortunately, deterrence often revolves around appearances. In wartime it is important that ships, tanks and aircraft are at the right place at the right time in the right numbers, and that there is the fuel and the kit to make them operate properly. But in peacetime, surface appearances can account for much more than wartime effectiveness. This is true with both adversaries and allies. In the world of political choices one country will rarely tell an ally that it cannot actually make the forward commitments required because the money is to be spent on sustainability. Without pushing the distinction too far, there is a tendency in times of calm and peace for a preference for visible indications of reassurance, rather than the more intangible requirements of readiness. When a crisis comes, readiness suddenly becomes all-important and we regret the trade-offs made in the past.

The conclusion from all of this is that it is the strategic importance of the North, rather than the 'Forward Strategy', which will prompt a shift in emphasis. The corrective mechanisms of the Alliance will limit the significance of that shift, but a shift nonetheless there will be. However, there is one question that we did not allow to intrude over-much into our conference discussions yet is in the back of all our minds – resources. Certainly in the case of Britain, if we are talking about a shift in priorities we must recognize that the shift will be not so much in terms of doing more but in terms of *not* doing less. This can be seen in the internal UK policy debate over the future of the amphibious capability, especially with regard to the replacement of the assault ships *Fearless* and *Intrepid* in the 1990s. The battle has not been fought in terms of a greater capability than the UK has now, but largely in terms of maintaining an equivalent current capability into the future. It is unwise to kid ourselves that NATO is talking about doing more in the North; it is talking about doing just about the same; and those concerned with the North should be very grateful if that is what is achieved.

One of the interesting things that came out in the conference is that it has not been as useful as has been commonly suspected in the British Defence debate to talk about a 'continental' versus a 'maritime' strategy. The choices are never quite as simple or direct as we might expect. The first resort of the budgeteer under pressure is to give up sustainability, in a sense, by cutting back on training, fuel and stores and then to shift new programmes 'to the right'. I suspect one of the prices NATO may be paying may well be in the area of sustainability. Another possibly heretical thought to come out of this volume is that role specialization may be a bad idea. If it is useful for the Armed Forces of one country to have experience of the problems of another, NATO should encourage participation of servicemen from one region in the security arrangements of others; NATO ought to think more across frontiers and Flanks and Commands. Role specialization, however attractive in terms of the logic and rationalization, may well be unfortunate in its political consequences. It has been interesting to hear Scandinavians argue that instead of less countries being involved in Nordic security, they would really rather have more.

May I finally offer one idea related to Britain's air defence problems. The UK constitutes one of the more important air defence regions of NATO and this importance is increasing. Should Britain be expected to handle it itself? One imaginative approach with important implications for the Alliance, (not to mention for the two countries involved), would be to have squadrons of Luftwaffe (perhaps using the Tornado ADV) based in Britain assigned to the UK air defence in the region. However we think of role specialization in the future, this book has at least brought out the importance for the cohesion of the Alliance of sensitivity to each other's security interests and problems.

Index

Aaland Islands, 3
Allied (Command Europe) Mobile Force (AMF), 41, 53, 55, 69
Amphibious operations, 131–9, 160–1
Andersson, Sten, 10
Anti-Submarine Warfare (ASW), 40, 79, 100, 101, 102, 111–12
Arctic, 68, 79, 80, 149
    Soviet attitude to, 60
Atlantic, 51, 99

Baltic, 16, 22, 51, 53, 54, 99, 104
    defence of approaches to, 107–9, 133, 144–5, 152, 153–8, 160, 169
    importance of, 127
    Soviet attitudes to, 56, 60, 61
Barents Sea, 3, 16, 22, 58, 61, 79, 126
Bodström, Lennart, 10
Britain, 5, 15, 31
    amphibious capability, 81, 131–9, 165, 183
    defence of own base, 120–1
    defence policy of, 65–73, 81–2, 165–6
    economic policy of, 26
    importance of sea to, 67–8
    interest in Nordic area, 41, 71–2, 73, 83, 112, 114–16, 170–1, 180, 183–4
    naval role in North, 116–22
    politics of, 110
    role in Baltap, 155–8
    support for NATO, 66–7
Brundtland, Margrit, 11, 26

Canada, 81, 100
    CAST brigade, 41, 142
Carlson, Ingvar, 10, 26
Central Front, 42, 43
    in relation to North, 43, 46, 48, 53, 74–6, 82, 83, 97, 114–16, 122, 126, 140, 146–7, 149, 169
Chernobyl, 25, 178
Churchill, Sir Winston, 115, 131, 145
CONMAROPS, 177

Dam, Atli, 9, 14
Denmark, 3, 5, 7, 13, 15, 39, 43, 51, 58, 72, 76, 133, 159–61
    defence policy of, 12, 16–17, 27, 31, 36, 38, 80–1, 99, 133, 146–7, 151–2, 176–7
    fishing limits, 15–16
    politics of, 12, 24, 27

EFTA, 7, 17
European Communities (EC), relations with Nordic states, 4, 5, 8, 12, 13, 14, 17, 18, 29
Evensen, Jens, 16

Faeroe Islands, 3, 9, 12, 13, 68
    defence of, 14, 16, 31, 169, 172
    fishing limits, 15
    politics of, 14
Falklands campaign, 133, 134–5, 137, 142, 144, 180
Federal Republic of Germany, 38, 53, 61, 67, 68, 77, 133, 147
    attitude to North, 176
    defence policy of, 107
    role of navy, 99, 103–4, 105–9, 133
    role in defence of Baltap, 153–7, 162
Fieldhouse, Adm. Sir John, 71
Finland, 3, 5, 9, 15, 51, 72, 80
    defence policy of, 9, 26, 27, 36, 39, 55
    politics of, 9, 24
Finnmark, 35, 42, 55, 76, 86, 133, 147
Fjorde, Einar, 11

Index

GIUK gap, 3, 40, 68, 118, 149, 169, 170, 172, 181
Gotland, 31
Greenland, 3, 4, 12
  defence of, 13, 31, 173
  fishing limits, 15
  politics of, 13

Hallgrimsson, Geir, 14
Hansen, General Bull, 11–12
Holst, Johan Jørgen, 11

Iceland, 3, 5, 7, 9, 15, 39, 51, 68
  defence policy of, 14, 16, 27, 31, 36, 38, 171, 175
  fishing limits, 14, 15
  politics of, 14–15
  threats to, 31, 169
Intermediate Nuclear Forces (INF) talks, 17

Jan Mayen Island, 3, 15

Kattegat, 72, 83
Keflavik, 14, 171
Kekkonen, President Urho, 9, 16, 56
Koivisto, President, 9, 16
Kola Peninsula, 16, 42, 49, 53, 78, 84, 97, 101, 122, 160, 165–7

Lehman, John, 78, 161
Leningrad, 42, 76, 84, 136, 139

Maritime arms control, 58–9
Maritime jurisdiction problems, 15–16
Motzfeldt, Pastor Jonathan, 13

NATO, *passim*
  command structure, 18, 106, 137, 162, 168–9
  Nordic attitudes to, 3, 11, 12, 14, 15, 16, 17, 18, 27
  standing naval forces, 177
  strategy of, 169
  value of, 72
Netherlands, role in North, 148–50, 176

Nordic balance, 22, 72, 149
Nordic Council, 8
Nordic states, 3, 4, 15, 17, 18
  economic situation of, 4–7, 25
  defence policies of, 15–18, 21–7, 35–8
  political situation of, 7–15, 23–4, 29
North Sea, 22, 68, 108
Norway, 3, 4, 7, 15, 27, 43, 51, 58, 59, 78, 79, 83, 86, 159
  airfields, 71–2, 77–8, 79, 85–6, 100, 126, 132–3, 134, 135–6, 138–9, 168, 169–70
  campaign of 1940, 83, 84, 112, 114–15, 136, 145, 148–9, 160
  coastal waters, 15
  defence of, 48, 69, 112–13, 124, 133–9, 140, 142, 144, 147, 166, 169
  defence policy of, 11–12, 16–18, 31, 36, 38–9, 40–44, 61, 110–11
  fishing limits, 16
  politics of, 10–11, 24
  prestocking arrangements, 41
  relations with EC, 29
  Soviet attitude to, 53–7
Norwegian Sea, 22, 58, 59, 68, 69, 70, 73, 79, 86, 98, 99, 137, 165, 168
Nuclear Free Zone (NNFZ), 16–17, 18, 21, 25–27, 49–50

Ocean Safari, 102
Ogarkov, Marshal, 51, 125

Palme, Olof, 9, 10, 16, 24
Pershing missiles, 12
Pringle, General Sir Steuart, 115

Reagan, President, 18
Royal Navy, 66, 71, 118
  role in North, 117–22, 173–4
  submarines, 70, 119
  surface ships, 120–1

Scandinavia, *see* Nordic States
Schlüter, Paul, 12

Sea-launched cruise missiles (SLCMs), 49, 78–9, 80
Sea lines of communication, defence of, 31, 35, 39–40, 43, 53, 69, 117, 125, 169, 172–4, 180
Sondrestrom, 13
Soviet Navy, 71
  containment of in North, 95–6, 99–102, 116–17, 117–20, 182
  exercises, 61, 78
  Northern Fleet, 46, 52–3, 65, 69, 71, 114, 116, 167, 171, 172
  protection of SSBNs, 35, 40, 44–5, 46, 52, 58, 78, 79, 101–2, 121, 125–7, 180, 181–2
  submarines, 70, 71, 78, 111–13
  submarine intrusions into Swedish waters, 10, 23, 30–1
  threat to SLOCs, 39–40, 78, 105, 180, 181–2
Soviet Union, 16, 30, 31, 35, 65, 74, 84, 178, 179
  defence in Northern Europe, 42, 46, 51–7, 58
  importance of Nordic area to, 46, 49, 58, 59, 61, 84–5, 146–7, 179
  maritime frontiers of, 31, 56, 60, 179
  relations with Nordic countries, 36–8, 56–7
  security policy, 90–2, 166
  Spetsnaz forces, 42, 117
  Western containment of, 92–4, 104–6
Strategic Defence Initiative, (SDI), 11, 18, 71
Sustainability, 159–60, 183
Svalbard, 3, 15, 169, 172, 175–6
Sweden, 3, 4, 7, 9, 15, 53
  attitude to Soviet Union, 30
  defence policy of, 10, 16–17, 21–8, 31, 72, 80, 84–5, 99
  politics of, 9–10, 24
  relations with EC, 29–30
  submarine threat to, 10, 22–3, 30–1, 76

Talleraas, Anders, 12
Thule, 13
Trondelag, 84
Turner, Admiral Stansfield, 124, 144

UK/NL LF, 41, 68–9, 142, 150, 155, 160, 161–2, 166, 173
Unden, Foreign Minister, 21
United States of America, 31, 65, 70, 81, 91, 92, 165–6
  defence relationship with Nordic area, 41, 94–102
  importance of Nordic area to, 46, 59
  global commitments, 65–6, 122, 176, 178
  Nordic attitudes to, 4, 13, 29, 39, 177
United States Navy, 45, 71–2
  activities in North, 52, 70
  delays in arriving, 118–19
  Maritime Strategy, 45–6, 56, 65, 71, 94–8, 111–13, 122, 124–5, 125–7, 144, 167, 177, 180–1, 182, 183
  submarines, 70, 78

Watkins, Admiral James, 58, 78, 159, 167
Western European Union (WEU), 18
Willoch, Kaare, 10